firsts

Origins of Everyday Things That Changed the World

Wilson Casey

ALPHA

A member of Penguin Group (USA) Inc.

ALPHA BOOKS

Published by the Penguin Group

Penguin Group (USA) Inc., 375 Hudson Street, New York, New York 10014, USA

Penguin Group (Canada), 90 Eglinton Avenue East, Suite 700, Toronto, Ontario M4P 2Y3, Canada (a division of Pearson Penguin Canada Inc.)

Penguin Books Ltd., 80 Strand, London WC2R 0RL, England

Penguin Ireland, 25 St. Stephen's Green, Dublin 2, Ireland (a division of Penguin Books Ltd.)

Penguin Group (Australia), 250 Camberwell Road, Camberwell, Victoria 3124, Australia (a division of Pearson Australia Group Pty. Ltd.)

Penguin Books India Pvt. Ltd., 11 Community Centre, Panchsheel Park, New Delhi—110 017, India

Penguin Group (NZ), 67 Apollo Drive, Rosedale, North Shore, Auckland 1311, New Zealand (a division of Pearson New Zealand Ltd.)

Penguin Books (South Africa) (Pty.) Ltd., 24 Sturdee Avenue, Rosebank, Johannesburg 2196, South Africa

Penguin Books Ltd., Registered Offices: 80 Strand, London WC2R 0RL, England

International Standard Book Number: 978-1-59257-924-2
Library of Congress Catalog Card Number: 2009924914

11 10 09   8 7 6 5 4 3 2 1

Interpretation of the printing code: The rightmost number of the first series of numbers is the year of the book's printing; the rightmost number of the second series of numbers is the number of the book's printing. For example, a printing code of 09-1 shows that the first printing occurred in 2009.

Printed in the United States of America

Contents

Contents

Contents

Contents

Contents

Contents

Contents

X

Y

Z

■

Introduction

History is complicated—everyone is his or her own historian, and it's often difficult to convince people something other than what they believe is, indeed, true. In real estate, it's all about location, location, location. You could say that with "firsts," it's all about definition, definition, definition.

As a professional researcher, I was amazed at the varied stories I found around firsts. It seems that for every first I could think of—and I thought of more than 500 firsts for this book—there were numerous possible answers as to what came first. If I went to one source I thought highly reliable and then went to another I thought just as reliable, I found two entirely different scenarios. Who was first? Who was *really* first? That source said what? The other one said that? Is that source biased? At times, trying to find the true first was a tough call. Was Jerrie Cobb the first female astronaut? I say yes, because she successfully passed all three phases of the Mercury program tests. Others adamantly say no because she didn't actually fly in space.

Does this book provide the absolute definitive answers regarding firsts? Absolutely not, but every effort was made to do so. I found many myths, errors, and half-truths I had to decipher. At times, I found blatant lies from sources trying to push their hidden agendas. (Maybe next I'll write a book debunking many historical "facts.") The only plausible method to arrive at the true facts would be to hop in a time machine with a staff of qualified and objective bystander-experts armed with camcorders to document the historical events as they happened. As with any research, the information-gathering sources I used may contain errors that I've passed on, but the vast majorities of the contents of this book were derived from reliable, historical information pools and expert historians. While some of the entries do represent reasonable deductions, it's very possible that further research into unpublished accounts of events may disclose additional data.

Another difficulty in determining a true first is due to terminology. An airplane is an aircraft, for example, but so is a balloon; similarly, automobiles used to be called *motorcycles*, and motorcycles used to be called *automobiles*. Among other problems was the simultaneity of several variations of the same invention; the difference between the actual invention and its refinement or development, manufacture, and promotion, leading to conflicts in claims; the inaccuracy or dishonesty of some claims; and the inadequacy of many of the records accepted as documentation for the claims.

While assembling the firsts, I quickly came to realize that often a lot of people appeared responsible for the same invention, and that nobody knew for sure who did it first. For instance, more than 100,000 patents by many different people and companies were necessary before the first automobile as we know it hit the road. Inventions that took hold of society were rarely the result of a spontaneous flash of genius by one single person. More often, they were built on previous ideas and trials, of which no exact date or individual can always be attributed.

Most often it was either luck, curiosity, or necessity to improve something that led the inventors, trail-blazers, and other first-makers to earn a spot in this book. Of course, some were driven by sheer competition to be the first. Take for instance, Mr. Martin Cooper of Motorola. In 1973, he made the first public telephone call placed on a portable cellular phone. Who did he call? His rival, Mr. Joel Engel, at AT&T's Bell Labs.

Napoleon Bonaparte said, "History is nothing but a lie agreed upon." Let me expand on Napoleon's thoughts: "History is nothing but lies agreed upon by the people in charge at the time." History, to me, is both truth and illusion. The same realm of thought holds true for determining a first. The credit often went to the inventor with the best publicity agent, the first to process a patent, or the first to tell his local newspaper. Many times the real first was too engrossed in his or her work to market or advertise their developments. Sadly, in many cases those passionate folks got lost in the shuffle of history, without their due credit.

A crackpot is a person to be first with a new idea or invention—until it succeeds and then he or she is a creative genius. This book is sincerely dedicated to the real "first" innovators who did not get listed in history textbooks.

Wilson Casey
"Trivia" Guinness World Record Holder
Spartanburg, South Carolina

Acknowledgments

Many people helped make this book a reality, including but not limited to: the reference librarians of the Spartanburg County Public Library, Spartanburg, SC, and especially Mr. Derrick Lawson; the response team at the organization and website of www.GotQuestions.org; the U.S. Secret Service, research department, Washington, D.C.; Mr. Loren R. Anderson, president, Snowmobile Hall of Fame, St. Germain, WI; Mr. Tony Brooks, inspirational motivator, Oak Island, NC; Mr. Deane Brown, retired teacher, Spartanburg, SC; Ms. Nikki Busch, grants and reference librarian, University of Wisconsin-Madison, Madison, WI; my mother, the late Helen L. Casey, possessor of great literary talent and so much more, Woodruff, SC; Mr. Marc A. Catone, writer, www.groups.google.com/group/1960s, Ithaca, NY; Mr. Andy Clark, director of Flea Circus Research Library, London, England; Mr. Paul Dinas and Ms. Christy Wagner, editors at Alpha Books, New York City and Indianapolis; Mr. Peter Doyle, MENSA member, Widnes, Lancashire, England; Mr. Peter Elliott, senior keeper, Royal Air Force Museum, London, England; Mr. Dave Evans, Director Society of Fire Protection Engineers (SFPE), Bethesda, MD; Mr. Tom Genova, owner, www.tvhistory.tv, Dearborn, MI; Ms. Jane Holeman of www.kitefestival.com and Ms. Kay Buesing of www.worldkitemuseum.com, Long Beach, WA; Ms. Connie Hollar and Ms. Colleen Casey, special research assistants, Spartanburg, SC; Mr. Jean Jergensen, executive director, and Mr. Paul Peinado, communications coordinator, World Lottery Association, Basel, Switzerland; the late Mr. Glenn Kennington, sports researcher, Spartanburg, SC; Mrs. Karen Lawrence, vice president, Cat Fanciers' Association Foundation, Inc., Manasquan, NJ; Mr. Jona Lendering, researcher, www.Livius.org, Amsterdam, Holland; Mr. Morten Lund, founding editor, *Skiing Heritage*, Accord, NY; Mr. Mike Mangus, historical editor, www.ohiohistorycentral.org, Columbus, OH; Mr. Robert Marvy, William Marvy company, Inc., St. Paul, MN; Ms. Lynne Olver, editor the Food Timeline, www.foodtimeline.org, Randolph, NJ; Ms. Christina Ratliff, Potter's Wax Museum, St. Augustine, FL; Mr. Bruton Redding, researcher assistant, Spartanburg, SC; Ms. Rita Rosenkranz, literary agent, New York City; Ms. Meredith Semones, librarian, University of Central

Florida, Orlando, FL; Ms. Janice Stillman, editor of the *Old Farmer's Almanac*, Dublin, NH; Mr. Larry Thompson, chief of communication, and Dr. Thierry Vilboux, Ph.D., National Human Genome Research Institute, Bethesda, MD; Dr. Deno Trakas and Dr. Vivian Fisher (retired) of the English Department, Wofford College, Spartanburg, SC; Ms. Alejandra Vergara, project coordinator, World Lottery Association, Montreal, Canada; and Ms. Amanda Forchilli, Office of New York State Professions, Albany, New York.

Finally, I wish to add a special thanks to all those not listed who gave so unselfishly of themselves. I shall always value their friendship, wise counsel, and generosity.

3-D Movie

On September 27, 1922, the earliest confirmed three-dimensional (3-D) film, *The Power of Love*, premiered at the Ambassador Hotel Theater in Los Angeles. The approximately 1-hour film starred Eliot Sparling,

Barbara Bedford, Noah Beery, Aileen Manning, Albert Prisco, and John Herdman. The invited audience of "200 scientists, photographers, motion-picture experts, and newspaper men," according to *Popular Mechanics* magazine, wore anaglyph (3-D) glasses and continually applauded throughout the film, although a glare marred the experience for many viewers.

24-Hour Store

Few seem to agree on the first 24-hour store, except to say that a store by definition offers services and/or goods in a retail environment. In the summer of 1876, Al Swearingen opened the Gem Saloon and Dance Hall in Deadwood, South Dakota. To accommodate the onslaught of treasure-seekers rushing into the area hoping to strike and find gold, Swearingen's all-in-one bar, saloon, shop, gambling parlor, eatery, and house of ill repute regularly stayed open 24 hours, never closing to paying patrons or "store" customers. The following spring 1877, he expanded operations to the Gem Theatre and offered all-night stage shows.

911 System

The first 911 call was placed on February 16, 1968, in Haleyville, Alabama. It was made as a successful test call by the Alabama Speaker of the House, Rankin Fite, and answered by Congressman Tom Bevill. The ability to dial a single number to report emergencies was now a reality. This new emergency number had to be three numbers that were not in use as the first three numbers of any phone number or area code in the United States or Canada. The Federal Trade Commission along with AT&T originally announced plans to build the first 911 system in Huntington, Indiana. Bob Gallagher, president of Alabama Telephone, was annoyed that the independent phone industry had not been consulted first. Gallagher decided to beat AT&T to the punch and have the first 911 emergency service built in Alabama.

1,000-Game-Winning Division I Basketball Coach

On February 5, 2009, in Knoxville, Tennessee, Pat Summit of the University of Tennessee became the first Division I basketball coach, men's or women's, to win 1,000 career games. She coached her Lady Volunteers (or Vols) to a 73–43 victory over the University of Georgia Lady Bulldogs for her 1,000th career win. Coach Summit began coaching in 1974 and reached the victory milestone with all 1,000 wins at the same school. She has also coached her teams to 8 national championships, and may accomplish more.

Adhesive Tape

The world's first adhesive tape (now known as masking tape) was invented in 1925 by Richard G. Drew and his researchers at the 3M Company in Minnesota. This first adhesive tape was easily removed and, therefore, perfect to help autoworkers paint straight lines and make clean dividing lines on two-color paint jobs. The tape was sticky only around the sides, not in the middle. It was a 2-inch-wide tan paper strip backed with a light, pressure-sensitive adhesive.

Advertising Agency

The world's first advertising agency, the William Tayler Agency, was founded by British businessman William Tayler in London, England, in 1785 or 1786. Tayler kept lists, files, and records of newspapers in his area, and not only acted as a newspaper agent but also an agent to the country printers and booksellers by taking in advertisements, including full-page-size, for city businesses. Tayler guided the ad placements in various print mediums and London directories. When he conducted business for a negotiable but minimal handling fee, the first advertising agency's commission was accepted.

Advertising Jingle

Product advertisements with a musical tilt can be traced back to the 1920s, around the same time commercial radio came to the public. General Mills aired the world's first singing commercial jingle, "Have You Tried Wheaties?" as a radio spot on Christmas Eve 1926 in the Minneapolis–St. Paul, Minnesota, area. It featured four male singers, contained several lines of copy, and ended with, "So just try Wheaties, the best breakfast food in the land!" The jingle was an absolute sensation, and the singers were christened as "The Wheaties Quartet." General Mills went on to purchase nationwide commercial time for the catchy advertisement, and that first advertising jingle saved an otherwise failing brand of cereal.

Advice Column

"Dear Beatrice Fairfax" premiered on July 20, 1898, in the *New York Evening Journal* as the first "advice to the lovelorn" column. It was spearheaded by Marie Manning, who worked with two other women in what was known as the publication's "Hen Coop." The three had created the women's page, and one day in 1898, editor Arthur Brisbane brought them three letters from readers seeking advice about personal problems. Manning suggested a new column exclusively devoted to dispensing personal advice. Both she and Brisbane agreed that a pen name was in order. Marie Manning suggested "Beatrice Fairfax," after Dante's Beatrice and the Manning family's country place in Fairfax County, Virginia. That first advice column served as the staging ground for the later nationally syndicated sister act of Esther and Pauline Friedman, better known as "Ann Landers" and "Dear Abby" for a significant part of their long and successful careers.

Aerosol Spray

In 1926, Norwegian inventor Eric Rotheim discovered that a liquid could be housed in and sprayed from an aluminum can injected with a pressure-building gas or liquid. Rotheim's pressurized container had a valve with a lever that, when pressed, released the liquid contents. But it was Julian Seth Kahn of New York City who received a patent for the first reusable spray can on August 22, 1939, for an "apparatus for mixing a liquid with gas." Kahn's spray can of 1939 was equipped with an inexpensive reusable valve mechanism that, under controlled pressure, could dispense such items as insecticides, paints, and even whip cream through a constricted opening. It was the predecessor of the modern aerosol spray can.

African American Political Party National Chairman

On January 30, 2009, Michael Steele, a former Maryland lieutenant governor, was chosen as national chairman of the Republican Party to serve a 2-year term. He clinched the inner-party election with 91 votes (a majority of 85 committee members was needed). The Republicans chose Steele over four other candidates, and Steele replaced former chairman Mike Duncan. Previously, Steele had been the first African American elected to statewide office in Maryland in 2002. He is an attorney by trade.

African American President of the United States

On January 20, 2009, Barack Hussein Obama was sworn in as the 44th president of the United States at the 56th Presidential Inaugural in Washington, D.C. Obama was born August 4, 1961, in Honolulu, Hawaii. His father, Barack Obama Sr., was born of Luo ethnicity in Nyanza Province, Kenya, and his Caucasian mother, Ann Dunham, grew up in Wichita, Kansas. Obama's parents separated when he was 2 years old and later divorced. The Democrat senator from Chicago, Illinois, was elected president on November 4, 2008. Obama and his wife, the former Michelle Robinson, have two daughters, Malia and Natasha (Sasha).

Air-Raid Shelter

In 1915 and 1916, during World War I, a German dirigible known as the zeppelin raided eastern England and London more than 50 times, dropping bombs in an effort to destroy the morale of the population. Civilians did the best they could, using their cellars and basements as makeshift emergency shelters, during the bombings. Howard Moyer Gounder built the first air-raid shelter in the United States in Fleetwood, Pennsylvania. Completed on November 1, 1940, the shelter's stone walls were 18 inches thick and set in concrete that supported an 8-inch reinforced concrete roof that was weather conditioned with asphalt tar. The floors also were made of cement. Bunks on one inside wall accommodated six people, while a stove provided heating and cooking capabilities. A protected chimney in the rear provided ventilation. The shelter's entrance had heavy double doors, one opening inward and one opening outward, each with a small window.

Aircraft Carrier

Several accounts exist of aircraft carriers that were adapted and modified from conventional warships to see service in wartime. The most notable was the British warship HMS *Furious*, built in 1917, later modified, and in 1918, used to launch a successful attack on a German zeppelin airbase. However, an aircraft carrier is a warship designed (not modified) for the primary mission of deploying and recovering aircraft, so the *Ranger* was the actual first specifically designed and built aircraft carrier. It was constructed by the Newport News Shipbuilding and Drydock Company of Newport News, Virginia; launched on February 25, 1933; and placed into service at Norfolk, Virginia, on June 4, 1934. *Ranger*'s first captain was Arthur Leroy Bristol.

Airline

The world's first airline that operated with scheduled flights on airplanes, not zeppelins, was the St. Petersburg–Tampa (Florida) Airboat Line. The airline, which flew from January to May 1914, offered twice-a-day, six-days-a-week service across the bay between St. Petersburg and Tampa. Aircraft builder Thomas Benoist, pilot Tony Jannus, and salesman Percival Fansler launched the concept. The airline operated two Model Benoist 14 airboats and one Model 13, which was used for instruction. Each flight across the bay lasted about 22 minutes. The passenger fare was $5, and each passenger was given a 200-pound allowance, including any baggage. The first passenger was a former mayor of St. Petersburg, Abram C. Pheil, who purchased the first seat at an auction with a bid of $400. The airline's last official flight occurred on May 5, 1914, when the airline ceased operations. Profits declined after a town subsidy expired and seasonal residents had returned north. This first airline had no crashes, passenger injuries, or deaths.

Airline Meal

The first airline meal was served October 11, 1919, as an in-flight prepacked lunch box. It was onboard a modified WWI bomber of Britain's Handley Page Aircraft Company on its London-to-Paris flight. This new passenger division of the company called Handley Page Transport became the first airline to serve in-flight meals. Although served as lunch boxes, the meals were prepared and packed before taking off to be available to paying customers at 3 shillings each. Those first lunch boxes probably contained a sandwich, a piece of fruit such as an apple, and hot coffee or tea.

Another first occurred on August 26, 1919, when Handley Page Transport carried two women passengers on its airline service between England and France. The first kitchens for serving meals in flight were established by United Airlines in 1936.

Airline Ticket

The first ticket to fly on an airline with airplanes, not zeppelins, cost a walloping $400 and was used on January 1, 1914. The ticket was purchased at an auction by former St. Petersburg, Florida, mayor Abram C. Pheil. Pheil wanted to be on record as the first airline passenger and also to bolster profits for aircraft builder Thomas Benoist's St. Petersburg–Tampa Airboat Line. Famed pioneering pilot Tony Jannus safely flew the former mayor round-trip across the bay between St. Petersburg and Tampa. The flight was only 22 minutes one-way, but it was the experience of a lifetime for Pheil. Afterward, normal fare dropped to $5 per passenger. That $5 allowed the passenger a 200-pound allowance, including any baggage, same as that first $400 ticket.

Altar

Around 2500 B.C.E., Noah constructed the first altar. As described in Genesis 8:21–22, the outdoor altar was made of earth or unwrought stone and built in the mountains of Ararat (present-day Turkey, about 750 miles northeast of Jerusalem) after the Ark had come to rest following the Great Flood. Sticks of wood were placed on top of the altar, upon which Noah made burnt offerings of every clean beast and every clean fowl. According to Scripture, the altar gave off a sweet scent and pleased the Lord.

Aluminum Cookware

On February 23, 1886, Charles Martin Hall of Oberlin, Ohio, invented a simplified process for producing aluminum, a lightweight, rust-free metal with good thermal conductivity. Hall went to Pittsburgh in search of financial backers and channeled his procedure into a line of cast aluminum cookware called Wear-Ever. On April 2, 1889, Hall obtained a patent for producing aluminum electrically instead of chemically, thus reducing its costs. His cookware met with indifference until 1903, when

Wannamaker's department store in Philadelphia, Pennsylvania, allowed a demonstration of aluminum cookware's unique abilities. A chef made apple butter in a lightweight aluminum pan without the need to stir it. That one gesture made the cookware's popularity skyrocket. Soon aluminum pots and pans become standard kitchen equipment almost everywhere.

Ambulance Service

The Knights of St. John created the first "ambulances" during the Crusades of eleventh-century Europe. The early emergency workers received instruction in first-aid treatment from Arab and Greek doctors and then treated soldiers on both sides of the battlefield by bringing the wounded, usually via hammocks or by physically carrying them, to nearby tents for further treatment. The men who transported the wounded were commonly paid small rewards.

The first motorized ambulance came into being in 1899. Made and adapted in Chicago, it weighed about 1,600 pounds and could travel up to 16 miles an hour. Five businessmen donated it to Michael Reese Hospital.

Amphitheater Stadium

Around 50 B.C.E., Roman politician and high priest Gaius Scribonius Curio devised the concept of the first amphitheater. Until then, gladiatorial contests were held in open-area formats. To seat and accommodate spectators, Curio had two semicircular wooden stands built on a pivot. (It was really two theaters built back-to-back.) They could be pivoted or swiveled so that together they formed an oval with the audience inside. The next amphitheater, also made of wood, was built in 46 B.C.E. by Julius Caesar. Architectural engineering led the way for improvements to better support the weight of the spectators and protect the wood from being destroyed by fire. The first permanent stone amphitheater in Rome was built by Statilius Taurus in 29 B.C.E.

Analgesic Pain Pill

On January 1, 1915, German pharmaceutical manufacturer Bayer offered aspirin for the first time in tablet form, making it the first analgesic (antipain medicine) or painkiller in pill form. (Opium, the oldest painkiller known to man, dating to the times of Homer's 750 B.C.E. *Iliad*, was either smoked or inhaled.) In the few years prior to 1915, aspirin was available via powdered form in glass bottles. German chemist Felix Hoffmann had developed it in 1897 as a treatment for his father's arthritis. Another chemist, Arthur Eichengreen, also made significant contributions to the development of aspirin during this era. With the convenience of pill or tablet form, aspirin soon became the highest-selling analgesic medication in the world.

Anesthetic

As early as 1500 B.C.E., Egyptians used an elixir of opium to dull the senses of patients undergoing trepanning, an operation to relieve brain pressure by drilling a circular hole in the skull. Much later, the invention of ether, the first anesthetic, brought about the end of surgical pain. On March 30, 1842, Dr. Crawford Williamson Long of Jefferson, Georgia, applied ether gas under a towel to patient James M. Venable to numb him so he could painlessly remove a cystic tumor from the back of Venable's neck. The operation was a success, and Long's bill was $2.25 (25¢ for sulfuric ether and $2 for excising the tumor). In 1845, dentist Dr. Horace Wells demonstrated the use of ether during surgery for Harvard Medical School students. In 1846, he was credited as being the first to discover the use of ether as an anesthetic. (Dr. Long's successful use in 1842 wasn't reported until 1852, when the Georgia State Medical Society was informed.)

Animated Cartoon

The first animated cartoon was *A Good Beer*, created by French inventor Charles-Émile Reynaud. On October 28, 1892, at the Musee Grevin in Paris, Reynaud exhibited three short animated cartoon films, *A Good Beer, Poor Pete,* and *The Clown and His Dogs,* consisting of loops of 300 to 700 individually painted images on frames. He had hand-drawn his cartoons onto film paper, which he then projected to audiences using his Theatre Optique system, a device that created optical moving illusions, similar to modern film projectors. This first performance of all three animated cartoons, which lasted about 15 minutes, was known as *Pantomimes Lumineuses (Luminous Pantomimes).*

Antibiotic

The first substance recognized as an antibiotic or as an agent that destroys bacteria was penicillin. In 1928, Sir Alexander Fleming, a Scottish bacteriologist at London's St. Mary's Hospital, whose lab was often kept in disarray due to his workload, was straightening up a sink piled with Petri dishes (culture plates) when he noticed something strange. He found that a mold on a discarded culture plate had an antibacterial action. The mold was growing on the plate, but the area around the mold had no bacteria growing. It had killed the bacteria by interfering with cell wall growth. He called the mold *penicillium* and the chemical produced by it *penicillin.* Fleming really didn't realize what he had discovered, but his findings, written up in 1929, presented penicillin as a possible antibiotic.

Antitank Weapon

Antitank rifles were the first attempt at stopping a tank with a portable weapon. They needed to be quick to reload and easily carried by one man. The world's first antitank weapon was the 13.2mm Rifle Anti-Tank (Mauser), a German weapon created during World War I that first appeared in February 1918. German engineering originated the idea of using heavy caliber and high-velocity rifles to stop tanks, and they designed the world's first weapon for the sole purpose of destroying armored targets. The weapons were mass-produced by the Mauser Company at Oberdorf and were issued to antitank detachments. Despite being cumbersome, the 13.2mm Rifle Anti-Tank weapons were fairly effective against early tanks that were protected by no more than about ½ inch of armor plating.

Aqueduct

Although famously associated with the Romans, aqueducts, artificial channels to convey water from one location to another, were actually devised much earlier. On the orders of Sennacherib, King of Assyria, the first aqueduct of notable record appeared in 691 B.C.E. and was 34 miles (55km) long. It consisted of a single arched bridge 30 feet high over a valley 900 feet long and was built to carry water from a distant river, the Great Zab, to Assyria's capital city of Nineveh with its beautiful gardens. Built of limestone masonry, this first aqueduct demonstrated an understanding of siphons and basic hydraulic principles.

Area Code

In 1951, the first area code assigned for telephone customers was 201. It covered the entire state of New Jersey as part of the North American Numbering Plan. Although it was part of the original set of 3-digit area code telephone numbers assigned to the United States in 1947, this first 201 area code was not placed into service for customer-dialing calls until 1951. Before this, only long-distance operators used the codes. On November 10, 1951, the first directly dialed call was made from Englewood, New Jersey, to Alameda, California. Direct-dialing using area codes gradually spread throughout the country. By the mid-1960s, it was commonplace in many larger cities, as each 3-digit area code may contain up to 7,919,900 unique phone numbers. For uniformity and consistency, the first digit was a number between 2 and 9, and the second digit was either 0 or 1.

Art Exhibition

Although cave paintings were a form of communication and also an artful form of expression, it's difficult if not impossible to ascertain any definite firsts among them, let alone the dates of creation. The first public exhibition of art began on April 9, 1667, in the courtyard of the Palais-Royale in Paris, France, and ran until April 23, 1667. Local artists displayed their paintings and hand-crafted sculptures as organized by the Academie de Peinture et de Sculpture. The palace was royal property at the time and was used for courtly entertainment, including opera productions and cultural events. The art exhibitions became very popular, and beginning in 1671, they were held biennially in the Louvre. This allowed for more exhibitions with public awareness and attendance.

Artificial Gene

A gene is a unit of heredity that determines the characteristics an organism inherits from its parents. Dr. Hargobind Khorana, an Indian American scientist, was responsible for producing the first manmade or artificial gene in his laboratory at Massachusetts Institute of Technology (MIT) in 1970. It was created using transfer-ribonucleic acid and was a 207-base-pair chain identical to a virus gene. Six years later, Dr. Khorana and his team created a second artificial gene, this one remarkably capable of functioning in a living cell. This valuable effort laid the foundation for a future in which scientists could use artificial genes to manufacture important proteins or cure hereditary diseases in humans.

Artificial Insemination

In 1783, Lazzaro Spallanzani achieved the first recorded artificial insemination when he successfully transferred semen from a spaniel to a female hunting dog. The Italian biologist's experiments on dogs proved for the first time that both semen and an ovum were required, and there must be physical contact between the two, for an embryo to develop. That first successful artificial insemination experiment in Spallanzani's laboratory revolutionized the way scientists thought. Up until then, they had a very primitive understanding of conception largely based on how plants grew.

Artificial Organ

The human kidney was the first organ to be artificially approximated by a machine. Willem Kolff, a young Dutch physician, invented the artificial kidney in 1943, during World War II. From 1943 to 1945, he treated 16 patients with acute kidney failure but had little success. All that changed in 1945, when his drumlike contraption worked. A 67-year-old woman in a uremic coma regained consciousness after 11 hours of hemodialysis (blood filtering) with Kolff's dia-

lyzer. (Her first words out of the coma were, "I'm going to divorce my husband.") Kolff's invention, although crude, became the standard treatment for chronic kidney failure during the Eisenhower years, leading Dr. Willem Kolff to be known as "the father of dialysis."

Assembly Line

In 1901, Ransom Eli Olds was the first person to use the assembly line, a manufacturing process in which parts are added to a product in a sequential manner to create a finished product much faster than with handcrafting-type methods, in a commercial environment. His product: the Curved Dash Oldsmobile. In 1901, the Olds Motor Vehicle

Company of Lansing, Michigan, produced 425 cars and was the first high-volume automobile manufacturer of the day. Henry Ford of the Ford Motor Company in Detroit, Michigan, came more than a decade later with his conveyor (moving) assembly line and is often wrongly credited as utilizing the first assembly line.

Astronomer

Aristarchus of Samos (Alexandria), who lived approximately from 310 to 250 B.C.E., is often referred to as the "Copernicus of antiquity." Considered the world's first astronomer, he laid the foundation for much scientific examination of the heavens. Aristarchus suggested that the earth revolved around the sun and provided the first estimate of Earth to sun distance. He was also the first to propose a heliocentric universe with the sun at the center. Written from a geocentric point of view, his thesis on the sizes and distances of the sun and moon was a break-through in finding distances to objects in the universe. His methods, concepts, and laws of the heavenly orbs were used by later astronomers and mathematicians.

Athletic Club

The world's first amateur athletic club, founded in London, England, in 1866 mainly for track and field events, was applicably named the Amateur Athletic Club (AAC). John Chambers, an Eton and Cambridge graduate, and noted Oxford 1-mile race competitor Victor Albert Villiers formed the AAC. They organized a "counter-to-the-Olympics" group and published the world's first definition of an amateur athlete. The AAC did not define amateur and professional as we do today in terms of money or athletic profit; rather, its definition was mainly a question of social class. *Gentleman* and *amateur* were synonymous, while *professional* meant "working class." The AAC declared that men who were mechanics, artisans, or laborers were de facto "pros" and were barred from all amateur contests, which were reserved for "gentlemen," the ones who did no labor for a living.

ATM

On September 2, 1969, the first ATM (automated teller machine) opened for business, dispensing cash to customers at Chemical Bank in Rockville Center, Long Island, New York. This debut ATM, located in the bank's wall and available for walk-up customers, was only able to give out cash after a coded card was inserted into a slot on the unit. Several industrious folks had worked on earlier versions of the ATM, but Don Wetzel, an executive at Docutel, a Dallas, Texas, company that developed automated baggage-handling equipment, is credited for conceiving and implementing the process for the modern ATM. Wetzel came up with the idea while waiting in line as a customer at a Dallas bank. The other two inventors listed on the patent along with Wetzel were Tom Barnes, the chief mechanical engineer, and George Chastain, the electrical engineer. It took $5 million to develop the ATM.

Automobile

The automobile as we know it today was not invented in a single day by a single inventor. More than 100,000 worldwide patents created the modern automobile. In 1769, the first vehicle on record to move under its own power was designed by Frenchman Nicholas Joseph Cugnot and constructed by mechanic M. Brezin. This first automobile was powered by a steam engine and was used by the French Army to haul artillery. The vehicle could reach 2½ miles per hour on its three wheels and had to stop every 10 to 15 minutes to build up more steam power. Its two rear wheels were about the height of the average man, while the front wheel was smaller and attached to the steam engine and boiler. In 1771, Cugnot accidentally crashed one of his vehicles into a stone wall, making him the first to get into an automobile accident.

Ballet

On October 15, 1581, the *Ballet Comique de la Reine* (*The Comic Ballet of the Queen*) was performed in Paris at the court of King Henry II and Queen Catherine de Medici for the marriage of the queen's sister. This first ballet presented the ancient story of Circe, who had the magical power to turn men into beasts. The magnificent 5½-hour show was performed by entertainers and featured sets staged by Balthazar de Beaujoyeulx, a violinist and dancing master who was ballet's first great impresario. He had come from Italy to be Queen Catherine's chief musician, and to be sure the audience followed the storyline, Beaujoyeulx provided copies of the verses used in the ballet. The spectacle included instrumental music, singing, dancing, and spoken verse as well as spectacular costumes, scenery, and elaborate floor patterns created by lines and groups of dancers.

Ballpoint Pen

The first patent on a ballpoint pen was issued on October 30, 1888, to John J. Loud of Weymouth, Massachusetts. Loud was an American leather tanner and shoemaker whose invention featured a reservoir of ink and a roller ball that applied the thick ink to leather hides. The pen had a rotating small steel ball, held in place by a socket with its marking point capable of revolving in all directions. On the patent application, Loud said that such a pen would be excellent for writing on leather and fabric. He called it useful for marking on rough surfaces such as wood, coarse wrapping paper, and other articles. Although he made a few of his ballpoint pens, Loud did not commercially exploit them and allowed his patent to expire.

Bank Robbery

In 1302 and 1303, while Edward I was away fighting the Scots, Richard de Podelicote and his criminal gang, assisted by good monks gone bad, broke into the vaults of Westminster Abbey in London, England, and stole as much as they could take of the English Crown Jewels. This was the fist big bank raid in history. The vaults were believed to be the most secure depository in the country because they were protected by the Church and were physically located under Westminster Abbey. The gang, with insider help from the monks, initiated work on the robbery at Christmastime and commenced removing goods from the vaults over a period of several months. The robbery was not discovered until mid-May 1303. Upon capture, Richard de Podelicote, along with his gang and 40 monks from Westminster Abbey, were executed.

Bar Code

The universal product code (UPC), or bar code, was invented in 1948 by Bernard Silver, a graduate student of Drexel Institute in Philadelphia, Pennsylvania, along with Joseph Woodland, his partner. They developed a circular, bull's-eye-style code and received a patent in 1952 titled "Classifying apparatus and method." The patent described techniques for creating machine-readable item identification codes. The first UPC-marked item ever scanned at a retail checkout was a 10-pack of Wrigley's Juicy Fruit chewing gum at Marsh Supermarket in Troy, Ohio, on June 26, 1974. The gum was simply the first item the cashier picked up from the shopping cart full of various bar-coded items.

The straight-line bar code we know today came about in 1970, thanks to work by consulting firm McKinsey and Co. and the Uniform Grocery Product Code Council, an organization of leading trade grocery associations.

Barbed Wire

Single-strand barbed wire was first introduced in France in 1860, but only on a very limited scale. The first semi-successful form of the product, two-strand barbed wire, appeared in the United States in 1867 and was patented by blacksmith Michael Kelly in 1868. In 1873, Henry M. Rose patented his version of the two-strand type and exhibited it at a county fair in DeKalb, Illinois. American businessmen such as Joseph F. Glidden, Jacob Haish, and Isaac L. Ellwood were among the fair's attendees, and they took the barbed wire concept further and launched the barbed wire industry. Not only did they improve the product, but they also paired it with successful marketing and advertising. Glidden's U.S. patent was issued on November 24, 1874, and for his business savvy, he became known as "the father of barbed wire."

Barber Pole

In 1642 England, the first barber poles were really bloody rags on a stick or pole hung outside the barber's door to dry. Bloodletting, or the bleeding out of a disease, was one of the barber's principal duties. During their practice of "surgery," a white cloth was used as a wrap or bandage, and in those days of primitive sanitation, the cloth was used repeatedly. The barber/surgeon simply rinsed out the cloth and hung it on a pole in the doorway of the shop to dry. The bandages would often flop, blow, and twist together, forming a spiral pattern around the pole. This subsequently led to the painted red-and-white-striped barber's pole we know today.

Barbie Doll

The first Barbie doll debuted at the New York International Toy Fair on March 9, 1959 (Barbie's official birthday). Created by Ruth Handler, cofounder with her husband, Eliot, of Mattel, a toy company in El Segundo, California, the doll appeared in a black-and-white striped swimsuit with her signature ponytail. The doll was marketed as a "teen-age fashion model" and was available either as a blonde or brunette. Barbie came about because in the 1950s, Ruth Handler had noticed that her daughter, Barbara, preferred to play with dolls that resembled adults rather than babies. During that era, most three-dimensional dolls looked like newborns or small children. Handler pushed the Mattel directors in the direction of a three-dimensional adult-bodied doll after seeing the Lilli doll while on a trip to Germany. Handler named her doll Barbie after her daughter, Barbara. It sold for $3, and during the introductory year of 1959, 351,000 Barbie dolls sold.

Barometer

The first barometer for measuring atmospheric pressure was invented around 1644 in Florence, Italy, by Evangelista Torricelli, Galileo's secretary. Galileo had suggested that Torricelli use mercury in his vacuum experiments. Torricelli filled a 4-foot-long glass tube with mercury and turned it upside down into a bowl. The tube was sealed at one end and left open at the other. The mercury flowed partly into the bowl and left a vacuum at the sealed top of the glass tube. Some of the mercury did not escape the tube, and after daily observations, Torricelli realized that the mercury was rising and falling due to changes in the weather. Thus the first barometer, reacting to changes in atmospheric pressure, was born.

Baseball Card

The first true baseball card sets were issued beginning in 1886 by Goodwin and Company of New York City. They numbered several hundred and featured sepia-toned photographs of baseball players.

These cards were essentially photos glued to stiff cardboard backings and were popularly called the "Old Judge" cards because the photos were stationary, not action, shots. Some of the cards featured players posing in studio-created backgrounds with props. Action shots showing catches and batter swings were made using innovations such as a baseball suspended on a string, and in many instances, you could see the string in the photo. Other sets featured full-color lithographs of the game's top stars. These first and foremost cards were quite popular with a public that was increasingly interested in America's favorite pastime.

Baseball Glove

In 1870, Doug Allison, a catcher for the Cincinnati Red Stockings, used the first baseball glove in a game because of an injured left hand. That first glove was an adapted leather work glove without full fingers—a far cry from today's baseball gloves. It was flesh colored to be as inconspicuous as possible, and had a large, round opening in the back for ventilation. Small sheets or strips of leather were inserted into the glove for extra padding. It's difficult to pinpoint the exact first player to wear a glove for fielding purposes, but it's logical that the catcher would have been the first position player to wear one because he handled hundreds of pitches and dealt with foul tips. Although at first, wearing a glove labeled the player as a "sissy" by many, it slowly caught on to more and more players.

Baseball Stadium

The first stadium, or enclosed baseball park, opened on May 15, 1862, after proprietor William Cammeyer put a fence around the Union Grounds in Brooklyn, New York. (With the fence came the over-the-fence homerun; before then, batted balls hit between outfielders could seemingly roll forever.) This crude stadium's farthest outfield wall was 500 feet from home plate, and the right-field wall was 350 feet away. The stadium featured wooden bleachers (a fire hazard) behind home plate

21

and partially up the foul lines for spectators. The stadium's capacity was around 1,500, and on April 18, 1869, Union Grounds featured the first non-All-Star game that had a cover charge. Admission was 10¢, and the game featured local players. Onlookers and fans who didn't get to sit lined the outfield fences four and five deep. In winter, this first baseball stadium was used as an ice-skating rink.

Baseball Uniform

It was April 24, 1849, when the first professional team, the Knicker-bocker Base Ball Club of New York City (New York Knickerbockers), officially adopted team uniforms. Owner Alexander Cartwright chose white flannel shirts with a black collar, blue wool pantaloons (loose-fitting pants gathered at the ankle), and chip (straw) hats for his players to wear. It was a simple outfit, but the choice of wool had an underlying meaning. Cotton would have been less expensive and made more comfortable uniforms, but during this time, it was strongly associated with work clothing. Cotton was not fashionable and respectable dress. The early baseball clubs wanted to distance themselves from the working class. Wearing wool aligned the players with organizations of a higher status.

Battery

Around 250 B.C.E., the first battery was used by the Parthians who ruled Baghdad. Now famously called the "Baghdad battery," it was made of a clay jar (for support) about 5½ inches high and 3 inches in diameter with a 1½-inch opening at the top. Inside this opening, and held in place with asphalt, was a tube made of a copper sheet. This tube was sealed at the bottom with a copper disc held into place by more asphalt. An iron rod suspended from the asphalt lid hung down inside the center of the copper roll. The use of asphalt sealing indicates that the apparatus must have contained some liquid, most likely vinegar, which is acidic. The pottery jar and its contents, the world's first battery, successfully produced an electric current of approximately 1.5 volts. There are a couple fields of thought as to the use of this first electrical current, from enabling primitive jewelers to electroplate precious metals to assisting physicians in medical therapy.

Battleship

Admiral Yi Sun-shin of Korea invented the first armored battleship in 1592. It was called a Kobukson, or "turtle ship," because of its appearance and toughness. Its crew was usually 50 to 60 fighting marines and 70 oarsmen. Turtle ships were propelled by oars or sails or both and were decked with iron plates that deflected incoming cannon fire. Spikes and knives were attached to the armored plates to discourage enemies from boarding. The bow of the ship had a large iron ram in the shape of a dragon. The ship was equipped with at least five different types of cannons and guns that could be fired in any direction. For camouflaging purposes, clouds of sulfur smoke could be emitted through the bow's dragon head to obscure the ship's position in short-distance combat. These first battleships were pretty much impervious to any other weapons or seaworthy vessels of the time, and Admiral Yi Sun-shin initially had five turtle ships built.

Beauty Pageant

The first beauty contest was around 475 B.C.E. in Susa, the capital of Persia. The Persian king, Ahasuerus, also known as Xerxes I, became drunk one night and sent for his beautiful queen, Vashti, to appear at a royal banquet. She refused to come. Disgraced by her action, the king banished her, and held a beauty contest at Shushan, the palace, to find the most beautiful girl to become his new queen. Many fair young maidens gathered together for the king to judge, and the king chose a young Jewish girl called Esther. As winner of this first beauty pageant, she became queen and was showered with gifts and servants.

Beer

Beer is the first alcoholic beverage known to civilization, with mentions dating to thousands of years ago. Nearly every culture developed its own version of beer, using various grains like millet, maize, cassava, rice, and barley. It's not known when the first alcoholic beer was created, but it was the first product humans made from grain and water, even before they learned to make bread. The Egyptian texts of 1600 B.C.E. contained medical prescriptions calling for beer. In 1935, the first canned beers by Krueger went on sale in Richmond, Virginia.

Bicycle

In 1790, Comte Mede de Sivrac of France constructed a wooden scooter-like device with two wheels, no pedals, no brakes, and limited steering ability. Between the two wheels, the rider straddled a wooden seat. The top of this first bicycle was only about 30 inches above the ground, and the rider propelled himself by kicking the ground with his feet. Because there was no steering, the passenger had to lean and shift his weight to the left or right to turn. That helped a little, but skilled riders could turn the bicycle in transit by lifting the front wheel in a hopping or jumping motion. While the wheel was slightly off the ground, they shifted the bicycle into the direction they wanted to go. They, in fact, were doing the first-ever wheelies.

Bifocals

Around 1760, Benjamin Franklin of Philadelphia, Pennsylvania, created his "double spectacles," or bifocals. They were a combination of both concave and convex lenses for two types of vision correction: a top lens for distant viewing and a lower lens for reading. Franklin had become annoyed at having to keep up with two pairs of glasses, and his double spectacles remedied the problem. He equipped an eyeglass frame with lenses that consisted of two parts with different focusing powers. The semicircular glass lenses joined horizontally. The line separating the two lenses was evident, but the concept worked superbly. The upper and lower semicircles provided different magnification strength, and wearers only had to move their eyes up or down to see clearly, far or near.

Big-Box Store

In 1962, Thrifty Acres, the first big-box store, opened in Grand Rapids, Michigan. Meijer's pioneered the store as a hypermarket or superstore concept that offered both groceries and department store goods. This first big-box store is still in operation today at the corner of 28th Street and Kalamazoo and encompasses some 180,000 square feet. Meijer's had been founded as a supermarket in 1934 in Greenville, Michigan, by Dutch immigrant Hendrik Meijer. Meijer also trademarked the phrase "one stop shopping." Thrifty Acres was built with 6-inch-thick floors so that if the concept failed, the nongrocery half could be converted into an indoor car dealership.

Bikini

The bikini, under that name, made its first proper introduction to the world of fashion design on July 5, 1946, worn and displayed at a Paris fashion show by blond French model Micheline Bernardini. The first bikini was printed with images of newspapers and designed by Louis Reard, a mechanical engineer who dabbled in ideas for swimsuits. He called his two-piece swimsuit "four triangles of nothing," and sent out skywriters over the French Riviera with the message "Bikini—smaller than the smallest bathing suit in the world." That clever wording made the name *bikini* the official tag for the two-piece swimsuit. Only three weeks earlier, Jacques Heim, a fashion designer and beach shop owner in the French resort town Cannes, introduced his bikini-like swimsuit creation, the Atome. Heim also used skywriters, proclaiming the new Atome "the world's smallest bathing suit." Heim never called it "bikini"; Reard did.

Billiard Table

In 1470, King Louis XI of France ordered the first billiard table of record to be custom made. The king, along with other bureaucrats, wanted the game of croquet modified for indoor play on a table. Those fifteenth-century British and French aristocrats decided that bending over outdoors to play was too glorified. The first table's playing surface was a green cloth to resemble grass. The table was extremely large compared to modern billiard tables. Standing on the table to play was not permitted, and a simple barrier was placed around the edges. The balls were shoved rather than struck with a wooden stick through a wire gate just like croquet. Over time, the players began using the sides of the table to purposefully angle the balls into the gates.

Billionaire

On September 29, 1916, John Davison Rockefeller's net worth officially surpassed $1 billion, making him the world's first billionaire. Born in Richford, New York, he became an American industrialist and philanthropist who revolutionized the petroleum industry. In 1870, he founded the Standard Oil Company, and as gasoline grew in importance, Rockefeller's wealth soared. His empire grew as he bought out smaller oil companies, and eventually, Rockefeller's company controlled more than 90 percent of the American oil market. Many regard him as the richest man in history.

Bingo

The first game of bingo can be traced back to 1530 to an Italian version called *Lo Giuoco del Lotto D'Italia*, or The Clearance of the Lot of Italy. That early game featured 90 balls instead of the 75-ball version common today and was played in a weekly tournament for the purpose of increasing Italy's budget without imposing additional taxes. In 1929, bingo was first played in the United States at a carnival in Atlanta, Georgia. Dried beans were used as markers, and the game was known as beano. Its fun and popularity spread from there. At a New York party later in the year, Edwin Lowe, a toy salesman, overheard an overly excited tongue-tied lady yell out "Bingo!" instead of "Beano!" upon winning a game. Lowe developed and marketed the game with the new name bingo, and the phenomenon was born.

Biofuel

The first biofuel—a solid, liquid, or gas fuel derived from relatively recently dead biological material—was wood. Wood has been in use ever since man first discovered fire for cooking and heating.

The second most common type of biofuel is ethanol, a colorless liquid that's been used by humans since prehistory as the intoxicating ingredient of alcoholic beverages. Ethanol is made by fermenting plant sugars and distilling the alcohol, and can be blended with petroleum-based gasoline as a fuel to lower emissions and increase engine performance. Ethanol was first prepared synthetically in 1826 through the independent efforts of Englishman Henry Hennel and S. G. Sérullas in France.

Bird Banding

The first record of a metal band attached to a bird's leg was around 1595, when one of France's Henry IV's banded Peregrine falcons was lost while chasing and attacking a bustard (a bird with long legs, a round body, and a fairly short beak). The falcon showed up a day later in Malta—about 1,350 miles away!—nonchalantly eating goat cheese and figs. The bird averaged flying 56 miles an hour for 24 hours. Until that day, no one knew falcons had such range. The first records of bird banding in North America are those of John J. Audubon, the famous American naturalist and painter, in 1803.

Birth Control Pill

The first birth control pill, Enovid, was introduced in 1960 by G.D. Searle and Company. It came in two doses, 5 and 10 milligrams, and was delivered in a small bottle, much like all pill prescriptions of that time. Birth control pills were offered for approval to the Food and Drug Administration in 1957 as a means to treat menstrual disorders and infertility. It wasn't until 1960 that the manufacturer submitted the same oral contraceptive (Enovid) for approval to prevent conception and unwanted pregnancies. The first pill, G.D. Searle and Company's Enovid-10, contained 9.85 milligrams of the progestational hormone norethynodrel and 150 micrograms of the estrogenic hormone mestranol. That's about 10 times the progestin and 4 times the estrogen contained in today's birth control pills.

Black Hole Discovered

In the summer of 1972, the first object to be generally recognized as a black hole was discovered by 28-year-old Charles Thomas Bolton, a part-time faculty member at the University of Toronto, Canada. While observing a couple binary stars (two stars that orbit each other), he made his discovery. The black hole in question was the x-ray binary star Cygnus X-1, whose companion was HDE 226868. Bolton detected Cygnus X-1's presence at the center of the Milky Way by observing star HDE 226868 wobble as it orbited around a massive but collapsing "invisible star" (Cygnus X-1). He also observed the appearance of a stream of gas flowing from the star to Cygnus X-1, swirling around it at incredible speeds before vanishing. In 1967, John Wheeler, an American theoretical physicist, first applied the term *black hole* to these collapsing objects whose gravitational field is so intense that no electromagnetic radiation can escape, not even light.

Blockbuster Film

The term *blockbuster* probably stemmed from the crowds of people that flocked to see the premiere of *The Birth of a Nation*, directed by D. W. Griffith, on February 8, 1915, in Los Angeles, California. The huge crowds formed long lines around the *block* to get tickets. Based on two novels by Thomas F. Dixon Jr., the film was a 3-hour silent epic about the South in the aftermath of the Civil War. Griffith used innovative editing and production techniques to create an unprecedented display of visual, thought-provoking entertainment. Blockbuster crowds came to see the film, making it the biggest money earner in film history until 1937, when *Snow White and the Seven Dwarfs* claimed that title.

Blood Bank

In 1933, Soviet physician Sergey Yudin tried blood storage using cadaver blood at the Sklifosovsky Institute in Moscow. But it was on March 15, 1937, at Cook County Hospital in Chicago, Illinois, that the first blood bank to preserve blood for future use in transfusions was established. Bernard Fantus, director of therapeutics at the hospital, formulated a hospital laboratory that could preserve and store live donor blood and coined the term *blood bank* to describe it. Fantus had seen a need for blood storage to avoid transfusions having to go direct from donor to patient. Physicians had seen the effectiveness of transfusion therapy on the front lines of war and wanted blood available for treatment of their patients. The blood bank filled that lifesaving need.

In 1940, American Dr. Charles Drew was a pioneer in blood plasma preservation and organized the world's first blood bank drive, nick-named "Blood for Britain." He also established the first American Red Cross blood bank.

Blood Transfusion

From the 1300s, the Incas of Peru regularly practiced blood transfusions centuries before the Europeans invaded their land. In their ancient engraved records, the Ica Stones of Peru show evidence of blood vessels being connected from one human to another via crude tubes (hollowed-out reeds). The Incas understood the life forces of blood and that a lack of blood meant certain death. The Incas' crude live donor blood transfusions would have had minimal problems from incompatibility. Most all the South American Incas had the same blood type—O-positive, same as all the indigenous peoples of the Andean region during that time.

Blue Jeans

In 1853, the first blue jeans came into existence through the ingenuity of Levi Strauss. Strauss was a 24-year-old German immigrant who left New York for San Francisco with a small supply of dry goods to open a makeshift shop during the California gold rush. Shortly after setting up, a prospector asked Strauss what he was selling. Strauss told him he had rough canvas to use for tents and wagon covers. Story has it that the prospector told him he should have brought pants because there weren't any strong enough. Immediately, Strauss had the canvas made into waist overalls, which the gold miners liked, except they complained that the overalls tended to chafe. Strauss substituted a twilled cloth from France called *serge de Nîmes* that later became known as denim. The pants were nicknamed blue jeans.

Bourbon Whiskey

In 1783, Evan Williams established the first commercial distillery, Old Evan Williams Distillery, to produce bourbon whiskey in the Commonwealth of Kentucky on the east side of what later became 5th Street in Louisville. Although others were individually concocting their own versions of bourbon whiskey, Williams took a professional approach to emphasize quality. A premium whiskey was his means to better the competition that would inevitably follow. Mother Nature smiled gracefully upon his efforts, too. The limestone water in the area used in the distilling process conveyed a particularly desirable taste for his product.

Bowling Alley

A "bowling alley" has recently been discovered in Al-Fayyoum governorate, south of Cairo, Egypt, dating from around 200 B.C.E. of the Ptolemaic Period. An Italian team unearthed a unique open structure in the area of Madi City (an ancient temple). Its smooth floor is composed of a single large block of limestone with a groove 4 inches deep and 8 inches wide. In the middle of the lane's floor there's a 5-inch-square hole. Two balls of polished limestone were found, one of which fits the groove while the other fits the square hole. This first bowling track is like no other discovered from the ancient world and was found next to the remains of a number of houses, each made of two rooms with a large hall. After considerable study, it's been proposed that this was the first attempt at the practice of bowling down an alley.

Box Spring

Very little is substantiated about the box springs first manufactured in France during the early to mid-1800s. On record, the first box spring to be imported to the United States from France was in 1857 by James Boyle of Chatham Square in New York City. He was a manufacturer of bedding who recognized the need for box springs to make mattresses less lumpy. These first box springs were about 12 inches deep and reversible. Their frames were made of lumber with spiral springs in eight sections joined together with strips of ticking. Twine also helped secure it all together. All-metal box springs came later, and it wasn't until the 1930s that box springs enjoyed wide use.

Boxing World Champ

On August 29, 1885, John L. Sullivan of Roxbury, Massachusetts, out-pointed Dominic McCaffrey of Pittsburgh, Pennsylvania, in Chester Park, Cincinnati, Ohio. The boxing bout was promoted "to decide the Marquess of Queensberry glove contest for the championship of the world," according to press at the time, and was boxing's first "heavy-weight" title fight with 3-ounce gloves and 3-minute rounds. Sullivan weighed in at 205 pounds to McCaffrey's 160. Sullivan was 5'10¼" tall; McCaffrey was 5'8½". By aggressively throwing more punches and scoring the most points, Sullivan won a six-round decision. (Some say the bout went seven rounds, as the referee had lost count.) Nicknamed the "Boston Strongboy," Sullivan was the first American sports hero to become a national celebrity. He was also the first American athlete to earn more than $1 million.

Braille Encoding

Approximately 500 years before Frenchman Louis Braille devised his encoding system in 1821, a Syrian Muslim created his own method of reading by touching raised letters of the alphabet, very similar to what Braille would later develop. In the fourteenth century, Zain-Din al Amidi was a blind scholar and distinguished professor at the University of Moustansiryeh in what is now Iraq. Although he went blind soon after his birth, he later improvised a method by which he identified his books and made notes to express to others. Zain-Din al Amidi was the first to utilize "touch reading," and used it to educate himself in law and foreign languages.

Brassiere

Around 2500 B.C.E., warrior Minoan women on the Greek isle of Crete began wearing and using a garment resembling a bra. It shoved their bare breasts upward and exposed them from their clothing. Hundreds of years later, the ancient Roman and Greek women strapped on a breast band to reduce their bust size. In 1907, the word *brassiere* was first reported in a copy of American *Vogue* magazine. The term came from the old French word for "upper arm" and appeared for the first time in the *Oxford English Dictionary* in 1912.

New York City socialite Mary Phelps Jacob devised the first modern bra with two handkerchiefs and some help from her maid. She earned a patent on November 3, 1914.

Breakfast Cereal

In 1863, Dr. James C. Jackson of Dansville, New York, a follower of Sylvester Graham (of graham cracker fame), developed the first ready-to-eat breakfast cereal. Granula, as Jackson called it, was graham flour dough baked into dry loaves, broken into chunks, baked again, and then ground into still smaller pieces. But it was far from convenient like today's breakfast cereals. It had to be soaked overnight before it was possible to chew the dense, bran-heavy nuggets.

In 1887, the next generation of breakfast cereals caught on when John Harvey Kellogg, operator of the Battle Creek (Michigan) Sanatorium, invented a ground wheat, oat, and cornmeal biscuit for his patients suffering from bowel problems. Kellogg initially called his cereal Granula but later changed the name to Granola after a lawsuit. His brother Will Kellogg later invented corn flakes and went on to found the Kellogg Company in 1906. By the 1930s, Kellogg's had invented the first puffed cereal and soon afterward introduced shredded cereal.

Breaking the Sound Barrier

In 1934, the first rocket of notable record broke the sound barrier. The ARS-4 was launched by the American Rocket Society from Marine Park, Staten Island, New York, on September 9, 1934. The unmanned rocket had a single thrust chamber with four angled nozzles. Its flight reached a speed over 700 miles per hour, a height of 400 feet, and a horizontal range of 1,600 feet. The ARS-4 rocket ended up in New York Bay. The American Rocket Society, originally founded on April 4, 1930, as the American Interplanetary Society, was a pioneer in designing and testing liquid-fuelled rockets and trail-blazed the path to the U.S. space program.

Brick

The first known bricks date to 7500 B.C.E. early Mesopotamia and were made from sun-dried clay mud in the Upper Tigris area of southeastern Turkey. Clay from deposits around the Tigris and Euphrates rivers was mixed with straw, shaped into individual bricklike units, and sun-dried (similar to the way kids make mud pies). These first mud bricks did not stand up to the tough weather conditions and were in constant

need of repair when used to construct primitive shelter. The first fired (cooked or heated) bricks were produced in the third millennium B.C.E. in Neolithic Jericho and were a much better product. The fired bricks meant more permanent buildings could be constructed in areas with high rainfall or with cold or very hot weather.

Broadway Musical

The earliest American musical for which a complete score and libretto survived was *The Archers*, also called *The Mountaineers of Switzerland*. It premiered in New York City on April 18, 1796, and ran for three performances at the John Street Theatre, east of Broadway. *The Archers* was a comic opera by librettist William Dunlap and composer Benjamin Carr. The musical was adapted from Friedrich von Schiller's William Tell legend and contrasted ideas of liberty and anarchy. It followed its initial three-performance run with two nights in Boston.

Bubble Gum

In 1928, the first marketable bubble gum was invented by 23-year-old Walter E. Diemer, an accountant with the Fleer chewing gum company in Philadelphia, Pennsylvania. Diemer spent his spare time playing around with new gum recipes and explained, in a 1996 interview with the *Lancaster Intelligencer Journal*, "I was doing something else and ended up with something with bubbles." Pink was the one and only shade of food coloring he had nearby, so his new bubble gum became pink. It was less sticky than regular chewing gum and also stretched more easily. Diemer carried a 5-pound glop of his new gum to a grocery store and conducted demonstrations. It sold out in a single afternoon, and before long, the Fleer chewing gum company was marketing and selling Diemer's creation, calling it Dubble Bubble.

Buddhist Monastery

Around 500 B.C.E., King Bimbisara of Magadha in India donated the great Veluvana Garden as a monastic dwelling to the future Buddha and the Order of Sangha. The Buddha humbly accepted the bamboo grove park because he wanted a residence that was secluded and quiet and not too far—nor too close—to the city. King Bimbisara was the Buddha's first Royal Patron, and it's said that as the king poured donation water for the facility, the earth quaked as if the main roots of Buddha's teachings had rooted into the ground. Even though the Buddha's new residence was known as Veluvanarama (*arama* is used to denote a monastery), there were no permanent buildings. The Buddha and his monks resided under the shelter of the trees for 6 years during the rainy season before moving elsewhere.

Bungee Jump

Around 1000 C.E., the first bungee jump was performed on Pentecost Island in the Pacific Archipelago of Vanuatu. A man called Tamalie in the village Bunlap had a quarrel with his wife. She ran away, climbed a tall Banyan tree, and wrapped her ankles with liana vines. Tamalie followed her up the tree. The woman jumped and survived because of the vines tied to her ankles. The man also jumped, not knowing what his wife had done. He died, and the men of Bunlap were very impressed by his performance. Thereafter, the jump transformed into an ongoing death-defying religious ritual called *naghol*, or "land diving," that inspired modern-day bungee jumping.

Burger Chain

In 1921, White Castle became the United States' first hamburger chain when Billy Ingram, a real estate businessman, and Walter Anderson, the man who first flattened hamburger into a patty with a spatula and grilled it on a bed of shredded onions, formed a partnership. With $700 borrowed money, the first White Castle opened in Wichita, Kansas, offering hamburgers at 5¢ apiece. The hamburger was considered low-class food before White Castle changed the public's mind through targeted ad campaigns. One PR initiative was printed coupons offering 5 White Castles (what the burgers were called) for 10¢. It also helped that the customers could watch the burgers being made. Ingram and Anderson came up with the 5-hole concept of burger-making to ensure the burgers were thoroughly cooked. In 1961, White Castle was the first chain to sell a billion hamburgers. White Castle's other firsts included the industrial-strength spatula, the mass-produced paper hat, and a marketing slogan for fast food; White Castle's was "Buy 'em by the sack." The founders of White Castle created a market demand for burgers and started many of the concepts still used in the fast-food industry today.

Button

Around 3500 B.C.E., the first buttons were used more as ornaments than as fastening devices. The earliest known buttons were found at Mohenjo-daro in India's Indus Valley. They were made of a curved shell and worn as a class status symbol. During that time, men used straps and pins to fasten their crude clothing while the first buttons just hung around, waiting for the next big clothing innovation. Later, around 700 B.C.E., the ancient Greeks and Etruscans used buttons made of wood, bone, or horn that fastened clothing via loops, not buttonholes. Fully functional buttons paired with buttonholes for fastening did not appear until the thirteenth century in Germany.

Cable Car

On March 23, 1858, Eleazer S. Gardner of Philadelphia, Pennsylvania, invented the first cable car and was granted patent #19736 for his "improvements in tracks for city railways." His cable streetcar was to run on an endless cable loop centrally housed in an underground tunnel with a series of pulleys inside. Gardner's conceptualization was not immediately put into practical use for transporting people. It was a few years later, in 1873, that Andrew Hallidie put his own cable car system into service on Clay Street in San Francisco, California. Both gentlemen's cable cars were based on the concept of placing a continuously moving wire rope in a conduit underneath a slot between the rails, all beneath the surface of the street. A gripping attachment connected to the cable car above could engage or disengage the cable to move the car. An engine in a centrally located powerhouse kept the cable in continuous motion.

Caesar Salad

The first Caesar salad was the 1924 creation of Italian immigrant Caesar Cardini, who had a small hotel in Tijuana, Mexico, not far from the California border. In the days of Prohibition, the Hollywood crowd and San Diego socialites would drive over the border to Tijuana to party, and they often wound up at Hotel Caesars for a meal before returning home. On July 4, 1924, an abundance of patrons arrived at Caesar's Hotel, sending the kitchen into a panic. There weren't enough fresh vegetables to go around, so Cardini concocted a salad he thought they'd really go for, and he would make it in public, tableside. Using basic ingredients found in every Italian kitchen, he used romaine lettuce, coddled eggs, garlic-flavored olive oil, Parmesan cheese, salt, pepper, and croutons flavored with Worcestershire sauce. Needless to say, it was a hit.

Caesarean Operation

Around 1500, the first woman, the wife of a pig gelding farmer, Jacob Nufer, in Sigershauffen, Switzerland, is reported to have survived through a caesarean operation of baby delivery, or C-section. Nufer was so distraught by his wife's prolonged labor that he felt no choice but to cut her open to somehow prevent his wife and baby from dying in childbirth. Utilizing his pig-butchering knowledge, Nufer successfully "operated" on his wife and delivered a healthy child who purportedly lived to the age of 77. Since ancient Roman times, the procedure had been performed only on the deceased or on women with little hope of surviving labor.

Calculator

In 1642, Blaise Pascal, a noted French mathematician, built the first mechanical adding machine or calculator. It was called the Pascaline and was based on a design described by Hero of Alexandria in the first century C.E. to figure a carriage's traveling distance. The metal device was about 14 inches long, 13 inches wide, and 3 inches high, about the size of a large shoe box. There were eight windows on its top, and through them could be seen a small drum with digits. In front of the windows, eight setting mechanisms enabled the user to enter numbers to compute. Although crude and tedious, the Pascaline could add, subtract, multiply, and divide. The basic principle of this first calculator is still used today in water meters and odometers.

Calendar

Many historians believe the first calendar was inscribed on a 30,000+-year-old bone known as the Blanchard Plaque discovered in Abri Blanchard, Dordogne, France, in 1879. Marks on the bone made by Paleolithic people represented sequential phases of the moon and were engraved based on observations over 9 weeks. The inscriptions on the plaque, small dots, are the oldest known use of numbers by humans.

Camera to Use Film Rolls

In June 1888, George Eastman of Rochester, New York, announced the Kodak No. 1, the world's first box camera to use roll film. Retailing for $25, it weighed 22 ounces and could take 100 (65mm) pictures. The shutter was set by pulling a string, and a V shape on top of the camera provided a sightline. After each exposure, the user manually turned a key on top of the camera to wind the film to the next frame. To develop the film, the user sent the entire camera back to the Kodak company. Kodak processed the film, reloaded the camera, and returned it to the user for a cost of $10.

Can Opener

In 1858, Ezra Warner of Waterbury, Connecticut, patented the first can opener, although some give the credit to Briton Robert Yeates's design. Warner's can opener was a crude gadget shaped like a bayonet and a sickle. The user jabbed the pointed bayonet part into the can and pushed it in up to a small metal guard that kept it from going in too much. At the same time, the sickle piece was forced into the can. The user had to saw up and down along the top edge of the can to open it. This first can opener was really hazardous to use but it became popular for grocers to have one in their stores to open customers' cans as they left the store. The U.S. military also used it during the Civil War, saving some bullets. (Previously, they had to shoot cans open.)

Canned Beer

On January 24, 1935, the first canned beer went on sale. Two thousand cans of Krueger's Finest Beer and Krueger's Cream Ale were delivered to faithful Krueger drinkers in Richmond, Virginia, as a test. The move was the result of a partnership between the American Can Company and the Gottfried Krueger Brewing Company. The can company also distributed can openers designed to punch a hole in the beer's lid, and the label was printed with a picture showing how to open the cans. Unlike with glass bottles, the purchase of canned beer did not require the consumer to pay a deposit. Ninety-one percent of drinkers approved of the new and first canned beer, which gave Krueger the green light for further production.

Canned Food

The first canning, or preserving, process was a product of the Napoleonic wars, when malnutrition ran rampant among the eighteenth-century French armed forces. As Napoleon prepared for his Russian campaign, he searched for a new and better means of preserving food for his troops and offered a prize of 12,000 francs to anyone who could find one. Nicolas Appert, a Parisian candy maker, was awarded the prize in 1809 for perfecting his idea of corking half-cooked food in glass sealed with wax reinforced by wire.

Cannon

The earliest known cannon was invented by Ctesibius of Alexandria in the third century B.C.E. It operated by using compressed air and was hundreds of years ahead of the Chinese with their crude, gunpowder-ignited cannons. Although little is known about the first compressed-air cannon, Ctesibius did mention it as an engine of war. Ctesibius's work on the elasticity of air was extremely important. He also invented the suction pump, the water clock, and the hydraulis (a musical instrument), all using compressed air. His work earned him the title "the father of pneumatics."

Carbonated Soft Drink

In 1807, the first flavored carbonated soft drink was made in Philadelphia, Pennsylvania, under the direction of Dr. Philip Syng Physick, who is also known as "the father of American surgery." Physick had ordered a chemist to prepare a carbonated drink with flavoring added as a possible remedy for an upset stomach. Although the type of flavoring wasn't documented, it was a soothing drink that pleased and helped the patient. It wasn't until 1832 that carbonated beverages gained popularity. That's when John Mathews invented an apparatus for making carbonated water and sold it to soda fountain owners.

Carhop

In the fall of 1921, the Pig Stand in Dallas, Texas, was the first restaurant to employ carhops. The term *carhop* came from the practice of a waitress or waiter jumping up on a patron's car's running board as the car pulled into the restaurant's parking lot. The carhops would take the order and then bring the food and drink out to the cars. Although dangerous at times, carhopping was found to be a very effective way of drawing customers to eating establishments, especially if the carhops were female rather than males. The first carhop probably delivered a Pig Sandwich and a frosty bottle of Dr. Pepper.

Caricature

Around 1580, the first caricatures known to have been drawn intentionally as individual works appeared, created by Annibale Carracci of Bologna, Italy. The word *caricature* is thought to have come from the Italian *caricare*, which means "to load," so Carracci's goal was to create images with as much meaning as possible. Another theory is that the word *caricature* was derived from Carracci's name. The first (or one of the first) caricature depicted a nude man who had climbed a tree and was picking grapes. Caricatures experienced their first successes in the closed aristocratic circles of Italy and France, where they were passed around for mutual enjoyment.

Cash Register

In 1879, the Ritty Model I was the world's first mechanical cash register. It was invented by saloon owner James Ritty of Dayton, Ohio, who devised the concept after seeing a tool that counted the revolutions of an ocean liner's propeller in its engine room. This first cash register was not electric powered and used metal taps with amount denominations pressed into them to indicate the amount of the sale. It also had a totals feature that summed up all the cash values of the keys pressed during a day. Another feature was the bell sound as the cash drawer opened when sales were rung up.

Casino

The oldest casino or gaming house in the world, the Casinò di Venezia, was established in Venice, Italy, in 1638. The casino opened in a district of Venice noted for its entertainment area and offered games and innovative amusement in a sumptuous environment. Built as an elegant palazzi, it was, and still is, a perfect example of aristocratic renaissance architecture. The first casino game played? A card game called faro that was further popularized by King Louis XIV in France.

Castle

Around 1400 B.C.E., the first walled city or castle complex was the biblical city Jericho. Located in the southern Jordan valley of Israel, Jericho was a walled city, complete with watch towers, in which more than a thousand people likely lived. The walls of this first castled city "came tumbling down" at the hands of the Israelites. An earthquake caused the complex's foundation and mud brick walls to crumble. The bricks fell into a pile at the base of the wall, forming a ramp that Joshua and his troops used to gain access to the now-defenseless castle.

Cat Show

In 1598, the earliest recorded cat show took place in England at the St. Giles Fair in Winchester. The event was a sideshow attraction at the fair, probably a spectacle not of beauty, but of beast. Live mice and rats were systematically released, and prizes were awarded for the "best ratter" and the "best mouser." A handful of cat entrants participated while onlookers gambled and drank.

Cataract Surgery

A cataract is an opaque film that covers the eye and affects sight, and the first cataract-removal surgery was performed by Indian physician Sushruta in the sixth century B.C.E. After the patient was given some relaxing herbs, Sushruta used a Jabamukhi Salaka, or a curved needle, to loosen the lens and push the cataract out of the field of vision. After these first cataract surgeries were performed, the eye was soaked with warm butter and then bandaged. Although the process was deemed successful, it was only performed when absolutely necessary.

Catcher's Mask

In 1876, an Ivy League man by the name of Fred Thayer invented the first catcher's mask. Thayer adapted a fencing mask for catcher Alexander Tyng of the Harvard Nine baseball team. This first catcher's mask, called a rat-trap, added protection and reduced the catcher's apprehension of being struck by the ball. Thayer immediately obtained a patent, and his mask was offered in the Spalding sporting goods catalog for the 1878 season. This first catcher's mask looked like a wire-basket cage with a vertical piece that ran between the eyes. It did have a little padding and a strap that went around the wearer's head to help hold it in place.

Celebrity Clothing Line

In the late 1950s, actor-turned-designer Richard Blackwell launched the House of Blackwell, and soon, he and his celebrity clothing line became synonymous. Mr. Blackwell was the first in history to present his clothing line on a television broadcast, called *Mr. Blackwell Presents*, and the first to make his line available for plus-size women. Blackwell offered fashionable dresses in the $800 to $1,000 price range and was designer to Yvonne DeCarlo, Jayne Mansfield, Dorothy Lamour, Jane Russell, Nancy Reagan, and others. Although a respected actor and designer, Blackwell is best remembered as a fashion journalist for his annual "Worst Dressed" list that named the biggest fashion disasters of the year.

Cell Phone

On April 3, 1973, on the streets of New York City, Martin Cooper, general manager of Motorola's Communications Systems Division in Chicago, Illinois, made the first public telephone call placed on a portable cellular phone. Who did he call? His rival, Joel Engel of AT&T's Bell Labs. Cooper had come to New York to demonstrate his new invention and connected to the area's telephone system through a base station he had installed in a Manhattan skyscraper. The first commercially marketed cell phone was 1983's Motorola DynaTAC 8000X. It cost $3,500.

Census Survey

On March 1, 1790, an act of Congress provided for the counting of all the residents of the United States to determine the number of representatives and amounts of taxes, authorizing the first organized census. The U.S.

Secretary of State at the time, Thomas Jefferson, was the nominal director of the first census. The law required that every household be visited on Census Day, August 2, 1790, and that completed census schedules be posted in two of the most public places within each jurisdiction. The result of the census was to be delivered to President George Washington. The 1790 census showed a population of 3,939,326 located in 16 states and the Ohio territory. Virginia came in as the most populated, with 747,610 residents, and Rhode Island was the least populous at 68,825.

Central Heating

Around 350 B.C.E., the Lakedaemonians (Spartans) of Greece had developed a central heating system for buildings. They warmed their floors from underneath using an arrangement of ceramic pipes that transported air that had been heated by an underground fire in a central location. The heat from the floors rose up to heat the rooms. Their method was the precursor to the ancient Roman hypocaust system that similarly moved air heated by furnaces through empty spaces under the floors and out of pipes in the walls.

Cheese in a Can

In 1966, Nabisco Company introduced Snack Mate, the first cheese in a can, with such flavors as American, cheddar, and pimento. Snack Mate was also referred to as aerosol cheese, but its container was not actually an aerosol spray can. The cheese was forced out of the can by an aerosol propellant, although the two products never came in contact within the can so it was safe to eat.

Cheeseburger

Many different sources claim the first hamburger, and the cheeseburger also has its share of steadfast beginnings. Most historians agree the first cheeseburger was created in 1924 when 16-year-old Lionel Clark

Sternberger (later proprietor of a Los Angeles–area steak house called The Rite Spot) experimentally dropped a slab of American cheese on a sizzling hamburger while helping out at his father's sandwich shop in Pasadena, California. Story has it that it was at the suggestion of a homeless man wanting to add a piece of cheese to his hamburger order. Sternberger liked it, and so did his dad, and the first cheeseburger—"cheese hamburger," as they called it—was born.

Chocolate Bar

In 1847, Joseph Fry produced the first chocolate bar in Fry's chocolate factory in Keynsham, near Bristol, England. Fry discovered a method of mixing melted cacao butter back into defatted cocoa powder. By blending in some sugar, Fry created a paste that could be pressed into a mold. After cooling, these molded chocolate bars became suitable for widespread consumption. These first bars, which Fry called *chocolat delicieux a manger*, or "eating chocolate," were immensely popular.

Chocolate-Chip Cookie

The first chocolate-chip cookie was conceived and invented in 1937 by Ruth Graves Wakefield, of Whitman, Massachusetts. Wakefield ran the Toll House Restaurant, and one of her favorite recipes was Butter Drop Do Cookies, which called for baker's chocolate. One day she found herself without baker's chocolate but with a bar of semisweet chocolate on hand. So she chopped it into pieces and stirred the chunks of chocolate into the cookie dough. Wakefield thought the chocolate would melt and spread throughout as the cookies baked, but she soon found out otherwise. The chocolate bits held their shape and created a sensation she called Toll House Crunch Cookies. The cookies soon became very popular, and Wakefield's recipe was published in papers throughout the New England area. In 1939, the cookie became nationally known when Betty Crocker used it in her radio series, "Famous Foods from Famous Eating Places."

Chopsticks

The widespread use of chopsticks has been traced to around 500 B.C.E. during the time of Confucius. (Although the first chopsticks may have been simple twigs used to spear a roast over an open fire 5,000 years ago.) The precise origins of using a pair of chopsticks to hold and take food to the mouth are unknown, but we do know they were invented in China. The chopsticks of Confucius's time were probably made of bamboo, and they paired well with the Chinese cooking method of cutting food into tiny pieces.

Christmas Card

John Calcott Horsley designed the first commercial Christmas card in 1843 in London, England. Wealthy businessman Sir Henry Cole, founder of the Victoria and Albert Museum, commissioned the design. The card was a picture of an old English festivity that showed a family toasting the season. One thousand cards were printed lithographically and hand painted by an artist named Mason. They were on a single piece of pasteboard measuring 5×3¼ inches and displayed the message, "A Merry Christmas and a Happy New Year to You." Cole used as many as he personally desired (around half) before selling the rest at 1 shilling each.

Circus

Circuses have been around since the time of the ancient Romans. Around 75 B.C.E., the emperor Pompey held spectacular shows full of lions, elephants, and chariot racing. These ancient circuses also featured slaves fighting to their deaths in quest of freedom and also dangerous duels with live animals. It was a spectacle of entertainment where the masses flocked to eagerly watch the happenings.

Civil Service Exam

Around 124 B.C.E. in ancient China, the Han dynasty introduced the first civil service exams. During this time, an imperial university and a system of schools were founded to teach Confucian political and social ideologies to students pursuing a career in government. Candidates were chosen by written examinations that took place over a series of days. Scribes copied potential students' answers to conceal the identity of the candidates from the examiners. The appointments to the schools were made, and the responsibilities were awarded based on demonstrated talent and ability. This was the first system of meritocracy.

Clock

Around 3000 B.C.E., the ancient Egyptians developed the first clocks in the form of sundials. To make the device, the Egyptians used *gnomons*,

or shadow sticks. These were vertical sticks, or stakes, placed in the ground and used to indicate time by the length and direction of their shadow. The Egyptians next developed a more advanced sundial by placing a T-shape bar in the ground. This device was calibrated to divide the interval between the sunrise and sunset into 12 parts.

Cloned Animal

Born on July 5, 1996, Dolly the Sheep was the world's first successfully cloned healthy animal. She lived until the age of 6 and was dubbed "the world's most famous sheep." The donor cell for the cloning was taken from a sheep's mammary gland. Using the process of nuclear transfer, it took 277 tries to effectively clone Dolly. The eventual successful cloning proved that a cell taken from a specific body part could re-create a whole individual. Ian Wilmut, Keith Campbell, and their colleagues at the Roslin Institute in Edinburgh, Scotland, facilitated the cloning process.

They had to take a cell, deprogram it, and then implant the resulting embryo. Dolly did not die from any deformations of cloning, by the way. It was progressive lung disease.

Closed-Captioned TV Show

On Sunday night, March 16, 1980, three networks officially offered closed-captioned television for the first time. On PBS, it was *Masterpiece Theatre*. On NBC, it was the Wonderful World of Disney's *Son of Flubber*. On ABC, it was the ABC Sunday Night Movie's *Semi-Tough*. The closed-captions were seen in households that had the first generation of the closed-caption decoder. That meant the viewers could see a transcription of the audio portion of the programming. The special device that permitted this was called the TeleCaption adapter. It was manufactured by Sanyo, sold by Sears for $250, and easily connected to a standard television set.

Coffee Bar

Kiva Han was the first coffee shop and bar; it opened in 1475 in Constantinople (now Istanbul), Turkey. The coffee was served strong, black, and unfiltered, a style introduced to the area by the Ottoman Turks. Kiva Han's coffee was brewed in an ibrik, a long-handled pot, and served piping hot to patrons. During this period, coffee was so important that it was legal for a woman to divorce her husband if he could not supply her with enough coffee.

Comic Book Superhero

In June 1938, Action Comics #1 came out with *Superman*. He was the brainchild of writer Jerry Siegel and artist Joseph Shuster. The cover of the comic book featured Superman in a red and blue costume lifting a car over his head. (Superman had powers far beyond that of a normal human being.) Siegel and Shuster had been pitching their Superman concept since 1933 and had been constantly rejected. But in 1938, the world first saw Superman with bullets bouncing off his chest. After all, he was more powerful than a locomotive and able to leap tall buildings with a single bound.

Comic Strip

In December 1903, *A. Piker Clerk* first appeared in the sports pages of William Randolph Hearst's *Chicago American* newspaper. This first comic strip printed in a daily paper was written and drawn by cartoonist Clare A. Briggs. The 6-days-a-week comic strip featured recurring characters in multiple panels. The storyline featured Mr. Clerk, a character with a gambling problem, who placed daily bets on a horse in the Chicago races. Even though the strip brought national fame to Briggs, it was cancelled in June 1904 because Hearst considered it vulgar.

Commercial Solar Energy

In 1939 and for years afterward, silicon solar cells were the first aspects of commercial solar energy. Although American inventor Charles Fritts invented the first working solar cell in 1884, the first commercial application didn't really gain possibilities until 1939. That was about the time of American engineer Russell Ohl's work with diodes, which led him to develop the first silicon solar cells. These cells allowed better conversion efficiencies of the sun's energy than earlier attempts. In 1946, Ohl received a patent for his "light sensitive device." As solar cells continued to improve, Bell Laboratories introduced the first space solar cells in 1950.

Computer

The Antikythera Mechanism dates from around the first century B.C.E. and is the most sophisticated mechanism known from the ancient world. The device has been proved to be an analog computer of sorts for modeling the solar and lunar cycles and predicting eclipses. This first computer was discovered in 1900 in an ancient shipwreck near the island of Antikythera, Greece. The mechanism had three main dials, one on the front and two on the back. It was comprised of numerous gears with the front dial having at least three hands, one showing the date and two others showing the positions of the sun and moon. The device is now understood to have been dedicated to tracking the cycles of the solar system.

On February 14, 1946, J. Presper Eckert Jr. and John W. Mauchly of the Moore School of Electrical Engineering at the University of Pennsylvania, Philadelphia, publicly demonstrated the ENIAC (Electronic Numerical Integrator and Computer). The device was housed in a 30×50-foot room, contained around 18,000 vacuum tubes, and required 130 kilowatts of power per hour to operate. Soon afterward it was used by the Army Ordinance Department at Aberdeen, Maryland, for calculations and data storage.

Computer Mouse

The world debut of the first computer mouse was on December 9, 1968, at the Fall Joint Computer Conference in San Francisco, California. The 1,000 or so computer professionals in attendance saw a live demonstration of the mouse by inventor Douglas C. Engelbart and a group of researchers from the Stanford Research Institute of Palo Alto, California. This first mouse was a 3-button hand-operated pointing device that enabled the computer user to manipulate text or images on a computer screen. It was originally referred to as an X-Y position indicator for a display system. On November 17, 1970, Engelbart was issued a patent for his computer mouse, so named because the "tail" came out the end.

Computer Virus

In the early 1970s, the Creeper computer virus was first detected on ARPAnet, a U.S. military computer network. The virus, written for the Tenex operating system, was capable of independently gaining access through a modem and could duplicate itself to remote systems. When it infected other networks, the taunt of "I'M THE CREEPER: CATCH ME IF YOU CAN" appeared. The Creeper was a malicious program that replicated itself to networked computers and deleted files. Its creator is still unknown. A copycat virus called the Reaper was released soon after the Creeper began making its rounds. The Reaper found the Creeper once inside the computer systems and destroyed it. Many think both programs were instigated by the same creator.

Concrete Highway

In 1891, the town of Bellefontaine, Ohio, experimented with the first concrete highway pavement project on sections of some of its roads, including Main Street. But it was 1909 when the Greenfield Township (now northwest Detroit) of Wayne County, Michigan, built the first mile of concrete highway on Woodward Avenue between Six and Seven Mile Roads. The first concrete highway was 1.2 miles long, 24 feet wide, 6.5 inches thick, and cost around $13,500. The success of this project furthered the development of modern automobile highways.

Contact Lenses

Believe it or not, in 1508, Leonardo da Vinci described and sketched the first ideas for contact lenses. An expert at optics and lenses, he described them as tiny removable lenses to be worn in contact with the eye, to rest directly on the cornea. Made of glass, the same as regular eyeglasses, the contact lenses would improve the wearer's vision. His notes and illustrations were meticulously inscribed *backward*, only to be read with the aid of a mirror. Although he envisioned the product and set the precedent for others, Leonardo da Vinci's contact lenses never came to fruition.

In 1801, Thomas Young, an English scientist and researcher, took the idea of the contact lens and made one to correct his own vision. His lens must have been terribly uncomfortable—it was a ¼-inch-long glass tube that was filled with water and strapped to his face.

Cookbook

A Sicilian Greek named Archestratus wrote the first known cookbook in 350 B.C.E. It was called *Hedypatheia*, which meant "pleasant living" or "life of luxury," and was recorded in classical Greek hexameters. The food in this first cookbook for "ones of the leisure class" was prepared in bite-size portions to be eaten without cutlery. (That probably meant a flat, pita-style bread for scooping up portions and a raised bread for absorbing soup.) The cookbook called for two courses. The first, or *deipnon*, was commonly strong-flavored appetizers served prior to the meat and fish dishes. The second, or *symposium*, was wine served with specially chosen flavors and food dishes to accompany the drinking session and entertainment.

Corporation

The Benedictine Order of the Catholic Church was the first corporation of any notable sort. It was founded in Italy around 529 C.E. by Saint Benedict and survives today. The order's *Rule of Saint Benedict* is a book of precepts written for monks living in the community. The solemn commitment of the monks is referred to as the "Benedictine vow," and includes the promise to remain in the same monastery with a conversion of manners, to practice chastity, and to show obedience to the superior. Benedict founded 12 such monasteries during his time, and they were governed by the same rules of order. This first corporation with its written-down bylaws became the standard for western Monasticism.

Correspondence School

The earliest effort of correspondence school, or distance education, appeared in 1728. Teacher Caleb Philips placed an ad in the March 20, 1728, *Boston Gazette:* "Caleb Philips, Teacher of the New Method of Short Hand" advertised that any "person in the country desirous to learn this art, may by having the several lessons sent weekly to them, be as perfectly as those that live in Boston." If you don't read 1728 English, Philips meant that by utilizing the then-new mail system, he would send weekly shorthand lessons to prospective students, thereby creating the first correspondence school.

Corset

Around 2100 B.C.E., both men and women wore the first corsets. They were invented on the Mediterranean island of Crete during the Minoan Bronze Age. The Minoans devised corsets that were fitted and laced tightly to better shape the human body. These first corsets were stiffened with ribs of copper and made of animal skins, the fresher the better, and worn not just for special occasions, but also daily use. Smaller versions, or corselettes, were also donned that left the breasts exposed.

Credit Card

In 1946, John C. Biggins of the Flatbush National Bank of Brooklyn in New York invented the first bank-issued credit card. Biggins was an innovative banker and consumer credit specialist who developed the first universal charge card plan, although it was limited in scope. His Charge-It program was a local community credit plan for a two-square-block neighborhood area near the bank. Participating merchants would deposit sales slips of the charged products and services into the bank, and the bank then billed the customer who had used the card. These first cards were not the plastic that's so common today, but instead were on paper stock that contained pertinent information. Biggins's Charge-It program was a convenience for the bank customers and a boom for the local merchants.

Croquet Set

In 1851, John Jaques and Sons, a London, England, sporting goods manufacturer, was the first to begin selling complete croquet sets. The first set was handmade, included four full-size hardwood ash mallets, a set of four challenge balls, challenge hoops, four croquet clips, ball markers, and a hand-painted winning post. Also included within the first set was a simplified rulebook that provided helpful hints on technique and the basic tactics of play. The company introduced the modern game of croquet in London at the Great Exhibition of 1851, the first World's Fair.

Cyber Café

In 1988, the Electronic Café International opened in Santa Monica, California, founded by American video artists Sherrie Rabinowitz and Kit Galloway. The multimedia artists had been employing cutting-edge technology in collaborative artistic works since the mid-1970s. The first cyber café offered a coffeehouse menu, computers with modems, other telecommunication equipment, and artistic events. By 1991, the Electronic Café International (ECI) had more than 30 networked affiliates around the world.

Dance Contest

In 1907, the first dance competition of note was held in Nice, France. Camille de Rhynal, a choreographer, dancer, and composer, organized the contest, a tango tournament. Records regarding the winners and the number of participants are sketchy, along with the criteria for judging, but it is recorded that this first dance contest was such a local success that de Rhynal held a similar tournament in Paris later that year. At the second contest, there was no split between amateurs and professionals, nor among representation of areas or locales. Competitors danced as couples, no matter their nationality. For example, the lady may have been French while the man was Spanish.

Day of American Television

The official first day of American television was Tuesday, July 1, 1941. (Any broadcasting before that date was considered experimental.) On that first day, the Federal Communications Commission (FCC) activated nonexperimental call letters for two stations: WCBW (later WCBS-TV) and WNBT (later WNBC-TV), both in New York City. Commercial advertising was permitted on the stations, and TV licenses were issued. Along with empty airings and test patterns, WNBT aired Dodgers versus Phillies baseball at Ebbets Field, and WCBW aired news, dancing lessons, and children's stories.

Daylight Saving Time

In 1784, the idea of a daylight saving program to make better use of daylight was first conceived by Benjamin Franklin during his stopover in Paris as an American delegate. In his April 26, 1784, essay, *An Economical Project*, Franklin wrote a whimsical discourse on the thrift of natural versus artificial lighting. He did the math on the substantial money (96,075,000 livre tournois, or about $200 million today) Paris could save per 6 months on candles and oil lamp use if a daylight saving plan was instigated. But it wasn't until April 30, 1916, that the first official daylight saving program began. On that date, at 11 P.M., Germany and Austria advanced the hands of their clocks 1 hour until the following October, when they set them back 1 hour again. The plan was not formally adopted in the United States until March 19, 1918.

Defibrillator

In 1947, thoracic surgeon Claude S. Beck from the University Hospitals in Cleveland, Ohio, first successfully applied defibrillation therapy and saved a human life. The patient was a 14-year-old boy, and the procedure was an open-chest defibrillation. The defibrillator used the alternating current from a power socket and transformed the surge to the heart by way of paddle-type electrodes. Several generations of scientists and clinicians worked to accumulate the knowledge that contributed to the success of cardiac shock therapy and finally led to the defibrillator Beck used.

Dental College

On February 1, 1840, the General Assembly of Maryland chartered the world's first dental college. Spearheaded by Dr. Horace Hayden and Dr. Chapin Harris, the Baltimore College of Dental Surgery was established in Baltimore. The college originated the Doctor of Dental Surgery (DDS) degree. Before that time, there were only about 300 trained and scientific dentists in the entire United States. Dr. Harris had come to Baltimore in 1830 to study under Dr. Hayden and then joined his mentor in his efforts to found the college.

Dental Floss

In his 1819 book *A Practical Guide to the Management of the Teeth*, American dentist Dr. Levi Spear Parmly discussed the first form of dental floss. Parmly described his invention, a homemade waxed string, as "The waxed silken thread, which, though simple, is to be passed through the interstices of the teeth, between their necks and the arches of the gum, to dislodge that irritating matter which no brush can remove, and which is the real source of disease." He also stated his belief that "a thread passed between the teeth after every meal will save more teeth from decay than all the brushes and powders that can be used where the waxed thread is neglected." Parmly sold his dental floss to his patients and to other dentists.

Dental Record of Forensic Evidence

In 49 B.C.E., the earliest-known example of forensic dentistry, the identification of human remains using dental evidence, involved Agrippina, the mother of Roman emperor Nero. Agrippina had ordered the death of her rival, Lollia Paulina, who was in competition with her to be the wife of Emperor Claudius. After Paulina's death, Agrippina demanded to see her head as proof of death. Agrippina wasn't sure her rival was dead until she identified Paulina's distinctively discolored front teeth.

Because teeth and dental structures may survive post mortem, identification by dental records is a reliable method still in use today. The procedure really began to take hold in 1924 and afterward, when August Vollmer, then chief of police in Los Angeles, California, implemented the first U.S. police crime laboratory.

Deodorant Soap

In 1894, Lifebuoy Royal Disinfectant Soap was launched in the United Kingdom. The soap was red, same as it is today. The name was later changed to Red Lifebuoy Deodorant Soap with the directions: "Add water to produce lather. Use as regular soap." Its popularity was the result of people beginning to seek out ways to improve their personal hygiene. Lifebuoy's advertising campaigns were also the first to use the phrase "body odor."

Detective Story

On April 20, 1841, the first detective story, *The Murders in the Rue Morgue*, was published. Written by American author Edgar Allen Poe, it featured the first fictional detective, Monsieur C. Auguste Dupin. The tale is narrated by the detective's roommate and is about Dupin's extraordinary ability to solve a series of murders in Paris. Through this first detective story, Poe introduced the concept of applying reason to crime solving to literature.

Dialysis Machine

In 1943, Dutch physician Willem J. Kolff invented the first practical artificial kidney dialysis machine called the Kolff Rotating Drum. Developed during World War II, the device used a 20-meter-long tube of cellophane casing as a dialyzing membrane. The tube was wrapped around a slatted wooden drum that was powered by an electric motor. As the drum revolved in a tank with dialyzing solution, the patient's blood was drawn through the cellophane tubing. This semipermeable membrane allowed for the toxins in the blood to be removed and diffused into the dialyzing solution. The cleansed blood was then returned via the circuit back into the body. These first dialysis procedures took around 6 hours to complete.

Dice

From around 3000 B.C.E., the first dice were used for fortune-telling, in religious divination ceremonies, for gaming, and for gambling. They were crudely made from the ankle bones, often called knucklebones, of sheep, llama, buffalo, and other hoofed animals. Some of the dice's sides contained markings, a precursor to numbering. The playing of

dice games probably originated in Egypt, where marked cubes have been found in ancient tombs. Some of these first dice were even altered for cheating. *Dicing*, as it was called, was a popular game. Dice were particularly significant to the ancients because gambling was an integral part of society.

Digital Camera

In December 1975, Steven Sasson, an Eastman Kodak Company engineer in Rochester, New York, made a successful working prototype of a digital still camera. His 8-pound toaster-size contraption captured a black-and-white image on a digital cassette at a resolution of .01 megapixels. Sasson and his chief technician, Jim Schueckler, persuaded a female lab assistant to pose for them. The image took 23 seconds to record onto the cassette and another 23 seconds to read off a playback unit onto a connected television. It popped up on the screen, and with some minor adjustments, the first digital camera still picture was deemed acceptable.

Digital Music

In 1951, the first known example of digital music made by a computer was a crackly recording made in Great Britain, when the British Broadcasting Corporation (BBC) recorded a musical performance for a children's radio show. The music was recorded on a Ferranti Mark I computer, whose short-term random access memory stored and played "God Save the King," "Baa Baa Black Sheep," and a short piece of Glenn Miller's "In the Mood." The computer was built by Ferranti, a UK electrical engineering firm, in collaboration with Manchester University. The Ferranti Mark I, capable of storing digital music, was also the world's first commercial computer; nine were sold between 1951 and 1957.

Diner

The first diner started in 1872 as a horse-drawn wagon equipped to serve hot food to employees of the *Providence* (Rhode Island) *Journal*. Walter Scott, an employee of the paper, ran the lunch wagon independently. He had previously supplemented his income by selling sandwiches and coffee to his fellow pressmen from baskets he prepared at home. Scott expanded on his idea and traveled factory-to-factory and business-to-business with his lunch-diner, selling inexpensive, quickly made food to the workers. Sample menu items from this first diner included boiled eggs, cut bread, and sliced chicken.

During the 1920s, the lunch wagon was more often called a diner because of its similarity to railroad dining cars. Also during the 1920s, the diner began to take on its classic form: a stationary restaurant that included booths.

Dinosaur Fossil

Although references to "dragon" bones were found in Wucheng, Sichuan, China, more than 2,000 years ago, the first dinosaur to be described scientifically was the Megalosaurus in 1824. William Buckland, an English geologist, paleontologist, and clergyman, first announced the discovery—the fossil bones of a giant reptile. He named the genus *Megalosaurus* and published his *Notice on the Megalosaurus*, or *Great Fossil Lizard of Stonesfield*, the first full account of what would later be called a dinosaur.

Disposable Diaper

In 1946, housewife Marion Donovan of Westport, Connecticut, unhappy with leaky, cloth diapers that had to be washed, invented the "boater," a plastic covering for cloth diapers made from a plastic shower curtain. In 1947, Donovan carried her ideas further, combining disposable, absorbent, paperlike material with her boater design, thus creating the first convenient, one-piece disposable diaper. But as a businesswoman in a man's world, potential manufacturers ridiculed Donovan, saying her disposable diaper was too expensive to market. Determined, she went into business herself. A few years later, in 1951, Donovan sold her company for $1 million to the Keko Corporation.

Disposable Tissue

In 1924, Kleenex facial tissues were first introduced, selling at 65¢ for a package of 100 soft paper sheets. The Kimberly-Clark Company, now of Dallas, Texas, was first to popularize the product. The facial tissues came into being after the company experimented with creped wadding for gas mask filters. The resulting product was originally marketed as a cold cream remover, but people used the tissue in many other ways, especially as a disposable handkerchief. After learning that many people were using the tissues to blow their noses, Kimberly-Clark began marketing the tissues as disposable handkerchiefs.

Dog Show

The first conformation dog show was held in Newcastle-upon-Tyne, England, on June 28 and 29, 1859. In a conformation show, judges familiar with specific dog breeds evaluate individual dogs for how well they conform to published breed standards. The 1859 show was the first that took preshow entries and offered a printed catalog of the contestants. Its organizers were two local sportsmen, and of the 60 hunting dogs who participated, all were pointers or setters. Prior to this show, there had been informal gatherings called Pot House Shows at which hunters could compare and discuss their dogs.

Draft

In the early first century B.C.E., ancient Rome first instigated a military draft. The early Roman legions were mixed volunteer and nonvolunteer enrolled units of available citizens over age 18 based on their property values. Raising the legions was an annual undertaking. The term of service was 1 year, although many of the same citizens were selected year after year. Local magistrates decided who in the tribes were to be presented for selection. If the circumstances of the state required it, the consuls could basically draft as many men as needed and abbreviate the recruitment process.

Drive-In Movie Theater

The Automobile Movie Theatre opened on Crescent Boulevard in Camden, New Jersey, on June 6, 1933. With an initial creation cost of $60,000, the theater was the brainchild of young Richard Hollingshead, who worked in his father's auto parts store. As a teen and into his 20s, Hollingshead experimented with his drive-in by placing a projector on the hood of his car and projecting a film onto a screen he'd nailed to trees in his backyard. He placed a radio behind the screen for sound. It took him a few years to perfect, but with his own funds and family help, he was able to bring his theater to life.

On opening night, the drive-in attracted 600 motorists to see the British comedy *Wife Beware!* starring Adolphe Menjou. The admission price was 25¢ per car and 25¢ per person, or $1 for a family. Three shows were offered at 8:30, 10:00, and 11:30 P.M. The first drive-in theater did not offer any in-car speakers. Instead, three large RCA Victor main speakers mounted next to the big screen broadcast the soundtrack.

Drive-Thru Restaurant

In 1926, the Maid-Rite Sandwich Shop of 118 N. Pasfield Street, Springfield, Illinois, was the first restaurant to offer drive-thru service. There was no speaker box to order through like modern drive-thru; instead, drivers pulled up to the window where orders were taken and processed, told the cook what they wanted, and then sat and waited in their vehicles for their food. The order would be prepared and then handed out the window with proper payment. The restaurant, which is still in business, was listed in 1984 on the National Register of Historic Places as the first drive-thru restaurant in the country. The first drive-thru order placed was probably the original Maid-Rite loose-meat sandwich and a root beer float.

DUI Arrest

On September 10, 1897, George Smith's swerving and eventual crashing of his cab into a building in London, England, was enough to make him the first person arrested for drunken driving. No one was seriously hurt, and Smith, a 25-year-old taxi driver, was formally charged at Marlborough Street Police Court for being drunk and in charge of an electric cab on Bond Street. He had violated a licensing act of 1872, which imposed penalties for being drunk on a highway or at other public places with any carriage, horse, cattle, or steam engine. Smith admitted to having consumed several drinks, was fined 25 shillings, and sent on his way.

E-Mail

In late 1971, computer engineer Ray Tomlinson at Bolt Beranek and Newman in Cambridge, Massachusetts, succeeded in sending a message from one computer to another via a network connection. The computers were literally side by side and joined with an ARPAnet (Advanced Research Projects Agency) connection, the basis of the modern Internet. Tomlinson sent a number of messages to himself from one machine to the other. He said that most likely the first message was "QWERTYUIOP" or something similar in all caps or "TESTING 1 2 3 4." For a marker to designate the network host, he chose the @ because it wasn't used in the spelling of a person's name. The @ was already a standard key on the older computer's keyboard; Tomlinson did not have to type Shift+2 to get it.

Earmuff

In the winter of 1873, young Chester Greenwood of Farmington, Maine, with the help of his grandmother, put together his earmuff device. Greenwood constructed the muff by bending some wire and then sewing on beaver fur for warmth covered by black velvet for comfort against the ear. Greenwood's first attempt worked, but he refined the materials somewhat because the ears flapped too much. By using a flat, ⅜-inch-wide spring steel band, he was able to attach a tiny hinge to each earflap. This allowed the muff to fit snugly against the ear and allowed the entire device to be coiled flat to be put away in a pocket. On March 13, 1877, 18-year-old Chester Greenwood was awarded patent #188,292 for his Greenwood Champion Ear Protector.

Easter-Egg Hunt

The custom of exchanging and rolling eggs began in ancient Egypt and Persia. In the 1500s, the Germans were the first to stage Easter-egg hunts. The German children waited all year long for the Easter-time appearance of the *Oschter Haws* (Easter bunny). Right before Easter, the children would run around making and hiding nests wherever they could—in barns, around in the yard, in their homes, etc.—in hopes the Oschter Haws would come and lay eggs in the nests. The adults would then secretly fill and place color-dyed eggs in the nests. On Easter morning, the children would eagerly jump out of bed to go on an Easter-egg hunt, checking the nests.

Electric Chair Execution

On August 6, 1890, at Auburn Prison in New York, William Kemmler, alias John Hart, was executed by electrocution in an electric chair in accordance with a law that went into effect January 1, 1889, allowing the use of electrocution. After Kemmler was strapped in, a charge of approximately 700 volts was delivered for only 17 seconds before the current failed. Kemmler was not dead though, and a second charge of 1,030 volts was applied for about 2 minutes, after which he was deceased. Kemmler had killed his lover, Matilda Ziegler, on March 29, 1889, with an axe and was convicted of first-degree murder.

Dr. Albert Southwick, a dentist in Buffalo, New York, first suggested electrocution as a humane means of execution. Although often credited with the invention of the first electric chair, Southwick was really more of a lobbyist who worked with New York Governor David B. Hill to help pass laws making execution by electricity legal.

Electric Guitar

Paul H. Tutmarc of Seattle, Washington, invented the first electric guitar in the winter of 1930–1931 in his basement workshop with collaborator Art J. Simpson. Borrowing an idea from a telephone's inner workings, the two created a transducer that converted one type of energy into another. They attached an iron blade with copper wire coiled around it to a large horseshoe-shape magnet. When it was placed in Tutmarc's flat-top Spanish-styled guitar and plugged into a converted

radio, the magnetic device picked up the instrument's sound and amplified it with beautiful tone. Unfortunately for Tutmarc, this first electric guitar later became overshadowed by others thanks to a combination of bad advice from patent attorneys and Tutmarc's own unfocused business interests.

Electric Light

In the first decade of the 1800s, English chemist Humphry Davy invented the first electric light, a controlled electric arc between two charcoal rods set 4 inches apart. The rods were attached to a 2,000-cell battery. After he connected the wires to his battery and pieces of carbon (charcoal rods), Davy discovered that electricity arced between the two carbon pieces and produced a hot, intense, and short-lived light. This electrical arc was the first electric light, and in 1810, Davy demonstrated his discovery to the Royal Institution of London.

Electric Motor

British scientist Michael Faraday developed the first electric motor in 1821. Faraday's invention demonstrated the conversion of electrical energy into mechanical energy by electromagnetic means. The first simple electric motor consisted of a free-hanging wire that dipped into a pool of mercury, where a permanent magnet was located. When a current was passed through the wire, the wire rotated around the magnet, which showed that the current gave rise to a circular magnetic field around the wire. The process proved that electricity and magnetism are connected. Based on his experiments, Faraday published his work on what he called electromagnetic rotation.

The first electric motor capable of a practical application was invented by British scientist William Sturgeon in 1832.

Electric Power Company

In October 1878, Thomas Edison established the Edison Electric Light Company, with the help of his friend Grosvenor Lowry at 65 Fifth Avenue in New York, New York. Other investors included the Vanderbilts and J. P. Morgan. To finance Edison's work, $300,000 was raised by selling 3,000 shares at a par value of $100 each. Half of the new company's shares went to Edison on the agreement that he'd work on developing an incandescent lighting system. In 1889, the company merged with several other Edison ventures to become the Edison General Electric Company.

Electric Toaster

The first electric toaster was the Eclipse. On the market in 1893, it was invented by the Crompton and Company of Chelmsford, Great Britain. The iron-wired device only toasted one side of the bread at a time and required the user to turn it off when the toast was ready. This first toaster never provided a consistent piece of toast, and burnt bread was a common result. The Eclipse eventually failed because its wiring easily melted, causing a fire hazard.

Element Discovered

In 1669, phosphorous was the first element discovered. Although elements such as copper, gold, lead, tin, mercury, iron, and silver have been known since antiquity, it wasn't until the seventeenth century that the first scientific discovery of an element was made. It occurred in Hamburg when German amateur alchemist Hennig Brand discovered phosphorous by boiling and filtering as many as 60 buckets of human urine. He was trying to manufacture gold, and by accident discovered phosphorous. The most interesting thing about the substance was that it glowed in the dark so brightly Brand was able to read by its light.

Elevator

Around 236 B.C.E., the first elevator was a freight elevator in ancient Greece. It was a platform raised by a system of pulleys and winches. A rope was wound on a revolving drum with handles, which was cranked to raise and lower the platform. There were no sides or top to the platform. These first elevators were used for hoisting loads during construction projects. They were devised and built by Greek mathematician, engineer, and inventor Archimedes of Syracuse (same person of Archimedes Screw fame).

Endangered Species List

On March 11, 1967, the U.S. Secretary of the Interior, Stewart L. Udall of Arizona, published the first official list of endangered species. Congress had passed the Endangered Species Preservation Act in 1966 after being inspired by the plight of the whooping crane. That first 1967 list was compiled after consulting the states, interested organizations, and individual scientists. The total listing was 78 species and included native fish and wildlife that were threatened with extinction. Among the first listed were the Indiana Bat (mammal), the Hawaiian dark-rumped petrel (bird), the American alligator (reptile and amphibian), and the shortnose sturgeon (fish). The list is updated annually.

English Novel

Composed around 1553 and printed in 1570 in London, William Baldwin's *Beware the Cat* was the earliest original piece of long prose fiction in English. The first English novel was a work of satirical anti-Catholic jaunts. Among them, this Dark Ages book gave rise to the idea that cats have nine lives with its phrase, "It is permitted for a witch to take her cat's body nine times." Other works lay claim to being the first English novel, notably *Le Morte d'Arthur*, written by Sir Thomas Malory and first published in 1485 by William Caxton. Most experts don't classify this work as a "novel" because it doesn't contain enough original material, so *Beware the Cat* gets credit as the first English novel.

Eraser

Around 1752, the first notable eraser was used at the eminent Académie Française (French Academy), which held meetings at the Louvre in Paris. The eraser was made of a natural substance called caoutchouc gum, an elastic, gummy substance obtained from the milky sap of euphorbiaceous trees. It was probably dried and heated somewhat so the immortels (members of the Academy) could hold it to erase errors, smudges, and other stray marks on their papers.

Escalator

On August 9, 1859, the first patent for an escalator-like machine was granted to Nathan Ames of Saugus, Massachusetts. Ames called his improvement on regular stairs "Revolving Stairs." His escalator was a giant triangle with steps mounted on a continuous belt or chain. The incline was at 45 degrees and came complete with handrails. One side was for riders going up, one side was for riders going down, and the upside-down bottom side ran under the surface of the floor. Although Ames died in 1865 before he could see a functioning escalator run, he was the first to show that a power-driven set of stairs could be used for transportation between floors or levels in buildings or in other places of pedestrian traffic.

Factory

Founded in Italy around 1104 C.E., the Venetian Arsenal was the first factory in the modern sense of the word—and several hundred years before the Industrial Revolution. The Venetian Arsenal, which employed 16,000 people, mass-produced ships on assembly lines using manufactured parts at a rate of nearly one ship every day and night. The shipyard and naval depot was one of the most important areas of Venice. Today it is a naval base, research center, and exhibition venue.

False Eyelashes

In 1916, movie director D. W. Griffith came up with makeshift false eyelashes to give actress Seena Owen a more dramatic appearance for the filming of the movie *Intolerance*. Griffith instructed a wigmaker to weave some human hair through fine gauze that was then adhered to the actress's eyelids. The lashes successfully made Owen's eyes larger than life. Unfortunately, Griffin did not patent the idea.

Fashion Show

In Cordoba, Spain, during the eighth century, Ali Ibn Nafi, otherwise known as Ziryab, introduced sophisticated clothing styles and the first fashion shows. The clothes were based on his inspirations and seasonal displays from his native Baghdad. The fashion shows were simple affairs at which he exhibited his wares brought from the Middle East to small groups. He had a lasting influence on fashion with his presentations that offered different clothing for mornings, afternoons, and evenings. Ziryab set the trends when each fashion was to be worn.

Fast-Food Restaurant

On June 12, 1902, the first Joseph Horn and Frank Hardart Automat opened in Philadelphia, Pennsylvania. Cafeteria-style prepared foods were available behind small glass windows and coin-operated slots. Food was served on real dishes with metal utensils, and drinks were served in glasses. Horn and Hardart opened another Automat in New York City at Broadway and 13th Street on July 7, 1912. Because of its popularity, the New York City Automat marked the real opening of the first fast-food restaurant. These restaurants popularized the concept of take-out food with the slogan "Less work for mother."

Fax

In 1843, Scottish clockmaker Alexander Bain received a British patent for "improvements in producing and regulating electric currents and improvements in timepieces and in electric printing and signal telegraphs"—or in layman terms, a fax machine. By combining parts from clock mechanisms and telegraph machines, Bain's first fax machine transmitter scanned a flat metal surface using a stylus mounted on a pendulum. The stylus produced back-and-forth line-by-line scanning and picked up crude images from the flat metal surface. It took another 100-plus years, and various improvements, for the fax machine to become popular.

FBI Agent

In 1908, the Federal Bureau of Investigation (FBI) originated from a group of special agents created by Attorney General Charles Bonaparte during Theodore Roosevelt's administration. The organization had neither a name nor an officially designated leader other than the attorney general, yet these former detectives, a number of Department of Justice personnel, and 10 Secret Service men were the first members of the FBI. On July 26, 1908, Attorney General Bonaparte ordered the 34 men to report to Chief Examiner Stanley W. Finch. This action is celebrated as the beginning of the FBI.

Female Astronaut

In 1960, Geraldyn M. "Jerrie" Cobb of Norman, Oklahoma, was the first woman to undergo and successfully pass all three phases of the Mercury astronaut tests. Along with other highly qualified ladies, Cobb had been chosen by the Mercury astronaut selection team. Nevertheless, as the first female astronaut, she was not allowed to fly in space. National Aeronautics and Space Administration (NASA) decision-makers at the time thought that furthering a special program for lady astronauts would be detrimental to the U.S. space program. On June 16, 1963, Valentina Tereshkova of the Yaroslavl region of the former USSR became the first woman in space.

Female Bullfighter

In January 1936, in the Plaza de Acho in Lima, Peru, Conchita Cintron became the first female public bullfighter. Recognized as the first woman to compete at a high professional level, she slew around 800 bulls during a 13-year career. Born in Chile in 1922, Cintron had originally trained as a *rejoneadora*, or horseback bullfighter. Cintron performed and was a big draw on the bullfighting circuit in Mexico, Portugal, southern France, Spain, and Venezuela, among others. Depending on the local laws, she was able to fight on foot as a *matadora* or on horseback as a *rejoneadora*.

Female Governor

On January 5, 1925, Nellie Tayloe Ross was sworn in as governor of Wyoming. She was elected on November 4, 1924, and was preceded in office by her late husband William B. Ross. Mr. Ross died from complications from an appendectomy on October 4, 1924, after about a year and a half in office. In the month after his death, the Democratic Party nominated his wife to run for governor in a special election. Nellie Tayloe Ross refused to campaign, but she easily won the race to become the first woman governor in the history of the United States. She narrowly lost her bid for reelection in 1926.

Female Judge

Around 1200 B.C.E., Deborah, wife of Lappidoth, became the first female judge. She was a Judge of Israel for 40 years during a time when judges ruled instead of kings. The Israelites came to her to decide their disputes, and she held court outdoors in Ephraim in a place called Deborah's Palm Tree. Deborah was a prophetess, judge, and military leader all in one. The accounts of Deborah are found in the Bible in Judges chapters 4 and 5.

Female Nobel Prize Winner

The first female Nobel Prize winner, Polish-French physicist Marie Curie, shared her 1903 Nobel Prize in Physics with Henri Becquerel and her husband, Pierre Curie. The three were given the award "in recognition of the extraordinary services they have rendered by their joint researches on the radiation phenomena." The award was split up, one half to Henri Becquerel, one fourth to Pierre Curie, and one fourth to Marie Curie. In 1911, Marie Curie also became the first woman to win the Nobel Prize in Chemistry, the first woman to be the sole winner of a Nobel Prize, and the first person to win a Nobel Prize twice.

Female Olympic Gold Medalist

The 1904 Summer Olympics in St. Louis, Missouri, was the first Olympics to officially award gold medals, and it was there that American Matilda Scott Howell became the first female gold medal recipient. She won for women's archery. In September 1904, the 44-year-old archer from Ohio won 3 gold medals for the events of Double National Round, Double Columbia Round, and Women's Team Round. Of the 651 athletes who competed in this Olympics, only 6 were women.

Female Olympic Individual Event Champion

The 1900 Summer Olympics in Paris, France, was the first Olympics in which women could compete, and it was there that Charlotte Reinagle Cooper became the first woman to win an Olympic individual champion title by capturing the women's tennis singles championship. Cooper, born in Ealing, Middlesex, England, wore an ankle-length dress in accordance with proper Victorian attire while she was playing, and she followed her singles victory by also winning the mixed doubles championship with partner Reginald Doherty. She didn't win a medal, though. Those weren't awarded until the 1904 Summer Olympics.

Female Professional Artist

Around 1552, the first female professional artist was Sofonisba Anguissola. She was an Italian Renaissance painter who was praised by Michelangelo himself for her drawing ability. Anguissola's self-portraits and family paintings earned her royal endorsements from the aristocracy of Milan, Mantua, Parma, and others. In 1559, she was invited to Spain to become a court portraitist for Philip II. Anguissola was also the first important woman artist of the Renaissance and the first female painter to enjoy an international reputation.

Female Sports Announcer, Radio

In the late 1930s and early 1940s, Mrs. Harry Johnson, whose first name was never recorded, was the first female sports announcer. She was heard over the radio in Omaha, Nebraska, accompanying her husband, who was the sports announcer for Central States Broadcasting. During the broadcasts of local high school sporting events, Mrs. Johnson provided insightful color commentary. She filled in airtime during lags in the sporting action and also helped keep statistics of the game to make a better sports broadcast. She and her husband made a great on-air team.

Female Sports Announcer, TV

In 1965, the San Diego, California–born Donna de Varona became the first female network sports announcer in television history when she signed a contract with ABC's *Wide World of Sports*. As a former Olympic athlete and champion, de Varona parlayed her sporting experience into broadcasting and traveled all over, temporarily filling in when regular anchormen became ill or went on vacation.

Female Supreme Court Judge

On September 25, 1981, Sandra Day O'Connor (born 1930) joined the U.S. Supreme Court as its 102nd justice and its first female judge. President Ronald Reagan had announced earlier, on July 7, 1981, that O'Connor was his appointee to fill a court vacancy. O'Connor was confirmed by a Judiciary Committee vote of 17 to 1 and won approval by the U.S. Senate by a vote of 99 to 0. She made it clear that the high court's role was to interpret the law, not to legislate. O'Connor served as an Associate Justice for more than 24 years until the swearing in of her replacement on January 31, 2006.

Ferris Wheel

In 1893, the world's first Ferris wheel was built for the World's Columbian Exposition held in Chicago. Pittsburgh, Pennsylvania, bridge builder George Washington Gale Ferris, who was greatly knowledgeable in structural steel, invented the amusement ride. The first Ferris wheel stood about 265 feet tall, weighed 1,200 tons, carried 36 cars, seated about 1,500 passengers, and sported 3,000 electric lights. It was an awesome display that was powered by two 1,000-horsepower engines. With its construction costs being roughly $400,000, Ferris's wheel certainly accomplished what the Chicago fair organizers wanted—something to rival the Eiffel Tower in Paris, France.

Fighter Plane

The Vickers F. B. 5 Gunbus was the first fighter plane. It was a two-seater bi-plane (two wings on each side) developed by the British Vickers company in 1914. As an experimental gun carrier, it had sufficient lift to carry a machine gun and its operator as well as the pilot. The gunner could fire the machine gun in a tiny forward compartment. Although this aircraft lacked speed, it was put into service over France in early 1915 during World War I.

Filibuster

On June 11, 1790, at Federal Hall in New York City, the first filibuster for the purpose of delaying legislative action occurred in the U.S. House of Representatives. Elbridge Gerry of Massachusetts and William Loughton Smith of South Carolina both made long speeches during that first U.S. Congress meeting. The resolution on the table was regarding the search for a permanent location for the federal government.

Financial Bubble

In February 1637, during the Dutch Golden Age, Dutch tulip contracts sold for more than 10 times the annual income of a skilled craftsman. During this period, contract prices for bulbs of a newly introduced tulip reached extraordinarily high levels and then suddenly collapsed. This economic rise and fall is generally considered the first recorded financial bubble, sometimes referred to as a speculative bubble, a market bubble, or a price bubble. "Tulip mania" is still often used to refer to a large economic bubble.

Fingerprint

Aside from prints found on ancient fossilized clay tablets, the first fingerprints used for identification purposes date from around 1859. William Herschel, a British magistrate at Jungipoor in colonial India, required that on any official papers, the "signers" had to add their palm and fingerprints for identification purposes. He is also responsible for the idea of police recording and using fingerprint records to catch repeat offenders. Herschel also collaborated with scientist Francis Galton to establish the first fingerprint classification system, which was implemented by Scotland Yard.

Fire Extinguisher

In 1722, German Zachary Greyl invented the first fire extinguishing machine and successfully demonstrated it in Paris, France, to the Secretary-at-War and others of influence. The device worked by suf-

focating out a fire. It consisted of a wooden vessel holding a considerable quantity of water. In its center was a fixed tube of gunpowder attached to a fuse. During a fire, the device was quickly wheeled into the flaming room or building and then the fuse to the gunpowder was lit. The resulting explosion was so forceful that it pushed the water into all parts of the room and extinguished most of the major flames.

Flamethrower

In the seventh century, *Greek fire* (a term coined later by western European crusaders in the thirteenth century) was projected upon enemy forces in the fashion of a modern flamethrower. The Greek fire was a weapon the Byzantines employed that was instrumental in saving Constantinople from invasions by Muslim fleets. Although previous incendiary weapons had existed, Greek fire was discharged from bronze tubes mounted on the prows of Byzantine ships. These first flamethrowers emitted a thunderous noise as they discharged. They were insidious, and the flaming discharge adhered to whatever it struck and couldn't be extinguished with water. The exact nature of Greek fire was a state secret known only to a small circle of Byzantine elites.

Flea Circus

In 1578, Mark Scaliot, a blacksmith and locksmith in London, England, exhibited the world's first flea performance to the London public. Scaliot skillfully devised a miniature lock of iron, steel, and brass composed of several pieces, including a pipe key. Along with it he fastened a very small 43-link chain of gold. All the items together weighed about $\frac{1}{10}$ gram. Scaliot put the device around the neck of a flea, and the flea pulled it with ease. From this demonstration of Scaliot's great craftsmanship, the "flea circus" had begun. Scaliot went on to expand this flea circus with more acts.

Fluorescent Lamp

In 1901, American inventor Peter Cooper Hewitt patented the first mercury vapor lamp, the prototype for today's fluorescent lamp. Hewitt, who built upon the work of the nineteenth-century German physicist

Julius Plucker and glassblower Heinrich Geissler, found that by passing an electric current through a glass tube containing tiny amounts of mercury, a bluish-green light was emitted. Exciting the mercury vapor created luminescence. Hewitt and George Westinghouse, another prolific inventor, formed Cooper Hewitt Electric Company in New York City to produce the first commercial fluorescent lamps for photographic studios and industrial use.

Fly-Fishing

Around 500 B.C.E., the Macedonians in the northernmost part of ancient Greece were perhaps the world's first fly fishermen. Their fishing was written about in the first century C.E. by Latin poet Marcus Valerius Martialis and in 200 C.E. by Roman author Claudius Aelianus. These authors wrote of people fishing in a river with a handmade fly. Aelianus described how the ancient Macedonians attached red wool and feathers to a hook. Their fishing rods (lacquered, sticklike poles) were about 6 feet long, which was the same length of the string attached with a snaring fly at the end.

Folding Stepladder

On January 7, 1862, John N. Balsley of Dayton, Ohio, patented the first folding stepladder. It was a wooden six-step device with an A-shape frame that could be folded or closed in behind the steps. (The steps themselves did not fold.) Balsley was a carpenter and inventor who replaced the typical ladder rungs with steps and attached the A-shape frame. The A-shape support behind the steps had a much wider base than the width of the steps, which provided stability. Previous to Balsley's invention, stepladders were not foldable for storage or ease of transporting.

Food Processor

The food processor is the brainchild of Pierre Verdan, a salesman in the early 1960s for a French catering company. Verdan noticed his commercial clients were spending a lot of time in the kitchen chopping, shredding, and mixing. His solution was a bowl with a revolving blade inside the base. In 1960, Verdan established Robot Coupe, a company to manufacture the first food processors, powered by industrial induction motors, for the catering industry. The food processor was not introduced to the domestic market until the 1970s.

Football Goalpost

On May 14, 1874, the first football goalposts were at Jarvis Field in Cambridge, Massachusetts, in a contest that pitted McGill University of Montreal against Harvard in a game of rugby football under Harvard rules. The goalposts were H-shape, constructed with two wooden upright posts, with a crossbar connecting them. The exact dimensions of these first goalposts are not well documented, but there was one goalpost at each end of the playing field. The game was also the first international rugby football contest as well as the first instance of an admission fee charged at a collegiate sporting event.

Football Helmet

In the 1893 Army-Navy football game, Admiral Joseph Mason Reeves (who would later be named "the father of carrier aviation") wore the first football helmet. It had been created by an Annapolis, Maryland, shoemaker after Reeves's navy doctor advised him that he risked death or "instant insanity" if he took another kick to the head. That first flimsy helmet with earflaps was crudely made of moleskin, but Reeves figured something on his head as protection was better than nothing. This helmet also served as the basis for early aviator caps.

Football Stadium

In July 1903, ground was broken for Harvard Stadium, the first stadium specifically built for American football. Located in the Allston neighborhood of Boston, Massachusetts, Harvard Stadium is a horseshoe-shape facility that was originally built by the Aberthaw Construction Company. The first football game played there was on November 14, 1903. Dartmouth defeated Harvard 11–0. The stadium's capacity at the time, including standing room, was near 40,000. It was also the first facility built primarily of concrete and the largest steel-reinforced concrete structure in the world at the time.

Forensic Autopsy

In 44 B.C.E., ancient Roman physician Antistius performed the first postmortem forensic examination in a criminal case as he comprehensively examined the dead body of Julius Caesar after his assassination. According to Antistius's autopsy report, he found that only 1 of Caesar's 23 stab wounds had proved fatal—the one to the chest. Antistius was Caesar's personal physician and the examining doctor of the case. This was history's first recorded application of medical knowledge to a homicide investigation.

Fork

The true origin of the fork is uncertain, but because the word *fork* comes from the Latin *furca*, for "pitch fork," it's likely the fork as an eating device dates to the days of ancient Greece, around 300 B.C.E.; the Romans followed shortly thereafter. Those early carving and serving forks were fairly large and made from animal bone. The Greeks' ingenuity soon allowed for hammered-metal forks with two tines. The use of the two-tined forks prevented meat from moving or twisting during carving. The metal forks used by ancient Greeks didn't make it to the Western world until around the tenth century.

Fortune Cookie

Despite the fact that they're often served in Asian restaurants, fortune cookies are actually an American invention that originated in California in the early 1900s. The well-known cookie is folded and baked around a piece of paper on which a saying, a series of lucky numbers, or a fortune is written. But who the actual inventor was, and in which California city they were initially developed, continue to be a matter of debate. One account has the cookie invented in 1914 in San Francisco by a Japanese immigrant named Makoto Hagiwara. His cookies included a thank you note inside and were displayed at the Panama-Pacific Exhibition at the 1915 San Francisco's World's Fair. Another account claims David Jung, founder of the Hong Kong Noodle Company, invented the cookie in Los Angeles in 1918.

Franchise

In 1932, Howard Johnson's opened the first business in what would become the Howard Johnson's franchise. The business, a restaurant in Cape Cod, Massachusetts, soon became known for its ice cream. The chain got its start in 1925 when Howard Dearing Johnson, the proprietor of a drugstore and eatery in Quincy, Massachusetts, started making homemade ice cream to sell at soda fountains. Unable to finance additional selling outlets on his own, he franchised the formulas for his ice cream and other specialties. Johnson's concept spread to hundreds of locations, and a central commissary supplied all the franchisees with food and ingredients so the quality remained consistent from franchise to franchise.

Fraternity

Aside from the guilds or sometimes-called fraternities of the Middle Ages, it was on December 5, 1776, that Phi Beta Kappa fraternity was founded at the College of William and Mary in Williamsburg, Virginia. This first American college fraternity was conceived by five young undergraduate men. At its first meeting on January 5, 1777, four additional men were selected to join and they, along with the five founders, were the first to obligate themselves to preserve the secrets of the fraternity. The group established a secret handshake, a ritual, a badge, and a motto that's remained unchanged: "Philosophy the Guide of Life."

Frisbee

In 1871, New England college students played with the first Frisbies. (The spelling would later change to *Frisbee*.) The students tossed and caught empty pie tins for fun and games. The tins bore the words *Frisbie's Pies* and had six small holes in a centered star pattern that produced a hum as the Frisbies flew through the air. The Frisbies were a by-product of the Frisbie Baking Company of Bridgeport, Connecticut, which produced and sold pies in the area. It wasn't until July 1958 that the Wham-O toy company officially marketed the Frisbee, an aerodynamically improved plastic version of the early Frisbie.

Frozen Food

On March 6, 1930, Clarence Birdseye made frozen foods a practical reality in Springfield, Massachusetts, when his products, the first retail frozen foods, were test-marketed in 18 retail outlets. Although frozen food has always existed in climates that were cold enough for the food to freeze, Birdseye found a way to flash-freeze foods and deliver them to the public. His first frozen foods included 18 cuts of meat, spinach, peas, fruits and berries, fish fillets, and Blue point oysters.

Game Show

In 1924, the first game show, *Pop Question*, aired on the radio, not on television. *Pop Question* was a news quiz sponsored by *Time* magazine. Roy Edward Larsen, who worked at the magazine, along with Briton Hadden, the cofounder, spearheaded the game show. Each *Pop Question* segment lasted 15 minutes, and questions were drawn from news broadcasts. A short time after they were asked, the answers would be given. Listeners played along at home, trying to come up with the correct answers before they were announced. *Pop Question* aired until 1925.

Garbage Bag

In 1950, Canadians Harry Wasylyk and Larry Hansen invented the green plastic garbage bag. These first green polyethylene garbage bags were intended for commercial rather than home use. The Winnipeg (Manitoba) General Hospital bought the first ones. The concept of disposable garbage bags caught on, and Wasylyk and Hansen were able to sell their invention to a big company, the Union Carbide Company in Lindsay, Ontario, where Hansen worked. The company later manufactured the bags under the name Glad Garbage Bags. They were for home use and first available in 1969.

Gas Engine

On May 25, 1844, Stuart Perry of New York patented the first engine using turpentine gas as fuel. Perry received an additional patent in 1846. (In addition to Perry's two patents, it's estimated that more than 100,000 patents went into creating the modern automobile.) Perry constructed an internal combustion engine with a two-cycle method of operation, and he also invented both air- and water-cooled gas engines.

Geisha

In Japan in 1589, the first geisha were male. The Taikomochi, as they were called, were the ringmasters of the brothel night life. They were expected to be extremely funny, and they loved to bring up taboo subjects for laughs. They performed their artful crafts within a walled quarter called Yanagimachi (Willow World). The first woman to call herself a geisha was Kikuya, a prostitute famous for her dancing, in 1750. The geisha had to rely on their talent as entertainers and had to follow strict rules. Any geisha accused of prostitution would be subject to an inquisition, which could result in her expulsion from the hanamachi (geisha district).

Genocide

During the fifth century B.C.E., King Ahasuerus (known also as Xerxes I) sent a decree by courier to every province in Persia. According to the Book of Esther 3:13 (King James Version), the decree ordered the local populations "to destroy, to kill, and to cause to perish, all Jews, both young and old, little children and women, in one day, even upon the thirteenth day of the twelfth month, which is the month Adar, and to take the spoil of them for a prey"—all because one man refused to bow to King Ahasuerus. The king later changed his mind, but because a royal decree could not be annulled, the king allowed the Jews to defend themselves during the attacks. Thousands were killed on both sides, but the Jews were saved from total destruction because of their piety.

Genome Map

Although there were earlier but incomplete statistical linkage maps, the first complete sequence of the human genome (an entire set of genes) was announced April 14, 2003, in Bethesda, Maryland. The map was the result of efforts of the International Human Genome Sequencing Consortium, led in the United States by the National Human Genome Research Institute and the Department of Energy, and sequenced the 3 billion DNA letters in the human genome. This international effort was one of the most ambitious scientific undertakings of all time.

Gentlemen's Club

In 1693, the first gentlemen's club, White's, was established. Italian immigrant Francesco Bianco (a.k.a. Francis White) founded the establishment at 4 Chesterfield Street in London, England. The club's original name was Mrs. White's Chocolate House because it sold hot chocolate— a rare, expensive commodity at the time. The club eventually converted into a fashionable and respectable gentlemen's club where members can come, relax, and discuss politics and other matters of the day. It's still in existence today. Prince Charles is among its famous members.

Germ Warfare

Around 575 B.C.E., the nomadic Scythians of the Black Sea used the first form of germ or biological warfare in the form of poison-tipped arrows. The Scythians had renowned skill with the bow and arrow and at times had served as mercenaries in Greek armies. They used the decomposed bodies of several venomous adders (snakes), mixed in human blood and dung, and sealed this into vessels, which they then buried until the mixture was sufficiently putrefied. During conflicts, they jabbed the tips of their arrows into the poisonous concoction and fired at their enemies up to 1,600 feet away at the rate of about 20 arrows per minute. When the poison-tipped arrows hit human targets, they infected the victim with the bacteria of gangrene and tetanus, while the snake venom attacked red blood cells and the nervous system.

Gideon Bible

On November 10, 1908, the first Gideon Bible was placed in a room at the Superior Hotel in Iron Mountain, Montana. Archie Bailey, a Gideon, was an accountant and a frequent guest at the hotel. He had earlier approached the hotel manager, Mrs. Edna Wilkinson, and asked for permission to place Bibles into the rooms. When Wilkinson agreed to his request, Bailey sent an order to the Gideon headquarters in Chicago, Illinois. Gideons International is a layman's organization formed in 1899. At their 1908 convention, the Gideons proposed that they "direct their energies toward furnishing a Bible for every guest room of hotels in the country." Gideons International still distributes Bibles to motels and hotels and have expanded their recipients to prisons, hospitals, and schools as well.

Glove

The ancient Egyptians were the first to use gloves around 1400 B.C.E. The crude, mittenlike hand coverings without finger holes were available in the shape of cloth bags with drawstrings at the wrist. Assistance from another person was needed to draw the strings. The nobility, clergy, and merchant classes often wore these first gloves, but Egyptian women also protected their hands with gloves during work and meal preparations. A linen pair of gloves was even discovered in the tomb of King Tutankhamen. Other gloves have also been discovered in the ancient pyramids of Egypt.

Gold Rush

Beginning in 1693, the first gold rush of note took place in the mountainous area of Minas Gerais in southeastern Brazil. It quickly became a major center of mining activities after the discovery of extensive gold and diamond deposits by the Bandeirantes, who were adventurers on slave-hunting expeditions. Between 1700 and 1800, nearly 1,000 tons of gold and 3 million carats of diamonds were mined from Minas Gerais. Thousands of slaves were brought in to work the mines and to do alluvial panning, a labor-intensive process. This first gold rush was punctuated by several clashes, the most serious being the Outsiders (Emboabas) War from 1707 to 1710.

Gold-Record Recording Artist

On February 10, 1942, as a publicity stunt to publicize the achievement of 1,000,000 record sales, RCA Victor presented Glenn Miller with a master copy of "Chattanooga Choo Choo" that had been sprayed with gold lacquer. The Glenn Miller Orchestra had performed "Chattanooga Choo Choo" in late 1941 in the movie *Sun Valley Serenade.* The movie faded, but the popularity of the song exploded. In fewer than 90 days, more than 1 million copies of the record sold.

Golf Course

As early as the mid-fifteenth century, men were playing golf on the Old Course at St. Andrews, Fife, Scotland. Although there were earlier games viewed as the ancestors of golf, the first permanent golf course originated at St. Andrews. On this first golf course, the holes were

placed according to where the rolling rough terrain allowed. The course had 11 holes laid out end to end. Golfers played the holes out and then turned around and played the holes in for a total of 22 holes. In 1754, the Royal and Ancient Golf Club, now known as the R. and A., was founded at St. Andrews.

Golf Tee

The first portable golf tee was patented by Scottish golfers William Bloxsom and Arthur Douglas in 1889. It was made of rubber and lay flat on the ground and had three vertical prongs to hold the ball in place.

This first golf tee did not pierce or peg the ground like modern tees and was certainly reusable. Originally, *tee* referred to the area where a golfer played, not the equipment used to elevate the ball. Before this first tee, to elevate the ball, golfers had to build a tiny mound of dirt or sand and balance the ball on top.

GORE-TEX Fabric

In 1969, Robert Gore and his father, Wilbert, of Newark, Delaware, discovered that polytetrafluoroethylene (PTFE) could be stretched to form a strong, porous material. The laminated fabric allowed water vapor to pass through while completely blocking water droplets. This was an extension of Wilbert Gore's work; he had been experimenting with insulation for electronic wires since 1958. The 1969 discovery came after the use of high temperature and a slow stretching technique. The Gores patented and trademarked their discovery as GORE-TEX. The fabric is commonly used in sports clothing.

Green Card

Originally called Alien Registration Receipt Cards, the first "green" card, #A1000000, was issued on August 1, 1940. It was a product of the Alien Registration Act of 1940 and was printed on white paper on Form AR-3. Passed as a national defense measure, the 1940 act required all noncitizens 14 years of age and older to register with the government. Registration, which occurred at post offices, included fingerprinting. The completed forms were forwarded to the Immigration and Naturalization Service (INS) for processing. Afterward, a receipt card was mailed to each registrant as proof of their compliance with the law. These first "green cards," however, did not discriminate between legal and illegal alien residents, but the program did intend to create a record of every noncitizen living within and/or entering the United States.

Greenhouse

The first greenhouse was built around 30 C.E. for the Roman emperor Tiberius. The specularium, as it was called, was an open house with walls built of stone above the ground. Fires were kept burning outside its walls to maintain the necessary heat inside. Glass had not yet been invented, so the structure's partial roof was painstakingly fabricated from tiny translucent sheets of mica. When Emperor Tiberius fell ill, his physicians ordered him to eat a cucumber-like fruit or vegetable every day. The cucumbers were planted in carts that were then wheeled out into the full sun every day and wheeled back into the greenhouse every night. Flowers and other fruits were also successfully produced in this first greenhouse, or as some early authors called it, cucumber house.

Grenade

Around 1231, the first grenade was used during the time of the Song dynasty. Invented by the Chinese, it was called *chen tien lei*, which meant "heaven-shaking thunder." The first grenades were packed gunpowder in ceramic and/or metal containers. When Mongol attackers were digging a tunnel to the base of a city wall, the Chinese soldier-defenders lowered a chain that held an iron can grenade filled with black powder. When it exploded, the grenade destroyed the tunnel and everyone in it.

Gun

Most historians agree that firearms originated in China in the 1100s C.E., thanks to a depiction of a gun discovered on a wall carving in a Buddhist cave in the Chinese province of Szechuan. The carving, which dates to around 1128 C.E., depicts a demonic warrior holding a bombard belching flames. Called a fire-lance, this first gun was a gunpowder-filled tube—probably bamboo—used as a flamethrower. Archaeologists also discovered a gun in Manchuria dating to the 1200s. It was more of a hand cannon that used some type of gunpowder formula to discharge its stone bullet. Although gunpowder dates to 850 C.E., its first use was in the making of fireworks because it didn't have the strength of gunpowder used in today's weapons. It took the Chinese a couple hundred years of experimenting and combining other substances with the early gunpowder to create crude hand cannons and exploding weapons or guns.

Hair Dye

As early as 3400 B.C.E., ancient Egyptians used henna, a shrub bush
with leaves that yield a reddish dye, to conceal their gray hair. They also
used henna to darken their nails and lips. Practically all ancient cultures
mention the use of hair colorings. These early hair dyes were made from
plants, metallic compounds, or a mixture of the two. The first synthetic
hair dye, called Aureole, came into commercial existence in 1909 by
the French chemist Eugene Schueller, who founded L'Oréal cosmetics
company.

Handheld Mirror

During the Bronze Age of approximately 3500 B.C.E., handheld mirrors
were first made and used in Sumeria and Egypt. The mirrors were not
made out of glass, but instead of metal sheets. Metals such as copper,
bronze, silver, and tin were flattened and polished until they were reflec-
tive and set into handles made of gold, wood, ivory, animal bone, and
other materials. These first mirrors were reserved for the royalty, but
used ones did eventually make their way out to the masses.

Hanging Death

According to Genesis 40:16–22 (King James Version), around 1747 B.C.E., Pharaoh's chief baker was the first person in written history to be

hanged. As the story goes, Joseph had interpreted the chief baker's dream: "Yet within three days shall Pharaoh lift up thy head from off thee, and shall hang thee on a tree, and the birds shall eat thy flesh from off thee." True enough, after 3 days, on Pharaoh's birthday, he hanged the chief baker.

Hearing Aid

In Europe in the mid-1600s, ear trumpets made of metal came into being. The cone-shape trumpet amplified sound down its narrowing tunnel end and into the ear. Various sizes and lengths were developed, shoulder straps were added for carrying, and many were painted black to better blend in with the user's clothing. A popular type was the London Dome used in the 1800s and early 1900s. Early man also used hollowed-out animal horns, stuck into the ear, to increase hearing abilities.

Hearse

Hearses were originally hand-drawn until horse-drawn makeshift carts were employed. Dating to 500 B.C.E., hearses conveyed the dead to a church or cemetery. In 1907 in Paris, although not heavily documented, silent electric motorized hearse vehicles were used at times. On January 15, 1909, a motorized petrol-driven hearse was used for the first time in a Chicago funeral procession when funeral director H. D. Ludlow broke from the tradition of the stately horse-drawn hearses that had been in use for centuries. Some of the first hearses also served as ambulances.

Heart Transplant

On December 3, 1967, surgeon Christiaan N. Barnard conducted the first human heart transplant. He and a team of doctors and skilled staff at Groote Schuur Hospital in Cape Town, South Africa, spent 9 hours transplanting the heart of 25-year-old auto crash victim Denise Darvall into Louis Washkansky, a retired dentist in his 50s. Washkansky lived for 18 days, until he succumbed to pneumonia. The drugs used to prevent his body from rejecting the new heart had weakened his resistance to infection, but his transplanted heart beat strongly to the end.

Helicopter Flight with Pilot

On November 13, 1907, at Coquainvilliers, France, French pioneer Paul Cornu first piloted a gasoline-powered twin-rotor craft of his own design. On his second attempt that day, he grabbed the undercarriage as his machine rose into the air and he and his brother tried to hold the craft down. Cornu jumped on one of the handles, and with one hand clinging to the undercarriage, he was able to reduce the aircraft's lift. Cornu flew as the makeshift pilot for a few short seconds about 6 feet off the ground. He landed on the ground without any damage to the machine or himself, and by a historical stretch, he did pilot the first noted helicopter's flight.

High Heel

According to many historians, the fashionable women at Knossos on the Mediterranean island of Crete wore a primitive version of high heels around 2100 B.C.E. The Minoan civilization of that era did use metal tools, and the culture exhibited a high degree of technological and aesthetic achievement. The high heels were crafted of animal horn and bone and strapped to the feet. Around 1600 C.E., high heels were (re)invented in France. Rather than a fashion piece, the French high heel was created in response to the problem of a horse rider's feet slipping forward in the stirrups while riding.

Hispanic Astronaut

In 1980, Costa Rica–born Franklin Chang-Diaz, a physics engineer, became the first Hispanic American astronaut. On January 12, 1986, Chang-Diaz became the first Hispanic American in space while onboard the STS-61-C, the *Columbia* space shuttle. During his 6-day flight, Chang-Diaz participated in the deployment of a satellite, conducted experiments in astrophysics, and operated the materials processing laboratory. He received the Liberty Medal, awarded to outstanding individuals chosen as representative of the most distinguished naturalized citizens of the United States, from President Ronald Reagan in 1986.

Ellen Lauri Ochoa became the first female Hispanic American astronaut in July 1991. On April 8, 1993, she became the first female Hispanic American in space while onboard the STS-56, the *Discovery* space shuttle.

Holding Company

The Nobel-Dynamite Trust Company of London, England, was the first international holding company, initiated by Alfred Nobel and his advisers in 1886. Previous to this, Nobel had various stocks and partial ownership interests in several companies, including blasting oil, dynamite, and gelatinized nitroglycerine explosives. Launching a holding company, a company whose purpose was to own shares in other companies in several countries and control and manage their joint business, was a new phenomenon in the business world. The Nobel-Dynamite Trust Company was formed by Nobel's holdings in British and German companies along with a number of independent German dynamite producers.

Hollywood Movie Studio

In the fall of 1911, Nestor Studios opened in the Blondeau Tavern building at the corner of Sunset Boulevard and Gower Street in Hollywood, California. This first Hollywood motion picture studio began business as an expansion of the Nestor Motion Picture Company of Bayonne, New Jersey, and was owned by brothers David and William Horsley. General manager Al Christie moved to California permanently to run the facility because the nice weather allowed year-round filming. The Horsley brothers remained back in New Jersey, where they handled the Hollywood studio's film processing and distribution. The studio had tremendous success with the slapstick *Mutt and Jeff* comedy films and with the westerns they churned out weekly. Other East Coast filmmakers soon flocked to Hollywood, and within a few short years, Nestor Studios, along with several others, merged with the new Universal Film Company.

Horse to Win the Triple Crown

Sir Barton, a chestnut thoroughbred colt, became the first winner of the American Triple Crown in 1919. At the Kentucky Derby, he led the field of 12 horses from start to finish, winning the race by 5 lengths. Just 4 days later, Sir Barton was in Baltimore and won the Preakness Stakes, again leading from start to finish. Sir Barton next won the Withers Stakes in New York. Shortly thereafter, he completed the first Triple Crown in U.S. history by easily winning the Belmont Stakes. Incredibly, Sir Barton's four wins were accomplished in a span of just 32 days. During the time, he was owned by Canadian businessman J. K. L. Ross and was in the hands of trainer H. Guy Bedwell and jockey Johnny Loftus.

Hovercraft

British engineer Christopher Cockerell invented the hovercraft in 1955. He developed the practical designs that led to the world's first man-carrying amphibious hovercraft, the SR.N1, to be produced commercially. At the end of May 1959, the 7-ton craft flew, but it wasn't until June 11 that it made its first public appearance over land and water in front of the world's press. The 20-foot craft was dubbed the "flying saucer," and within weeks, on July 25, the SR.N1 successfully crossed the English Channel.

Hydroelectric Plant

On September 30, 1882, the world's first hydroelectric power plant began operation on the Fox River in Appleton, Wisconsin. It was initiated by local paper manufacturer H. F. Rogers and later named the Appleton Edison Light Company. This first plant was an electricity-producing station that used the natural energy of the river. When it first opened, it was able to produce enough electricity to light the home of Rogers, the plant itself, and a nearby building.

Iditarod

In February 1967, the first short Iditarod Trail Sled Dog Race was held in Alaska. Fifty-eight dog mushers competed in two heats along an approximately 25-mile stretch of the old Iditarod Trail between Wasilla and Knik. A relatively unknown participant named Isaac Okleasik from Teller, Alaska, won with his team of large working dogs. A $25,000 purse was offered, and Joe and Violet Redington donated 1 acre of their land adjacent to the Iditarod Trail to help raise funds. The Aurora Dog Mushers Club, along with men from the Adult Camp in Sutton, Alaska, the Redingtons, and others, helped clear years of overgrowth from the trail in time to put on this first Iditarod. For his relentless dedication, Mr. Joe Redington is remembered as "the father of the Iditarod."

Immigrant to Pass Through Ellis Island

On January 1, 1892, Ellis Island officially opened, and on that day, an Irish girl named Annie Moore was the first registered passenger to pass through the immigration station. It was her birthday, too. She had just turned 15 and was presented with $10 for being the first person through the new station. Miss Moore was traveling with her two younger brothers, Anthony (11) and Phillip (7). They had departed from Queenstown, Ireland, on December 20, 1891, aboard the SS *Nevada*, spent 12 days at sea, and arrived in New York on New Year's Eve. Soon all three Moore children were reunited with their parents, who were already living in New York.

Income Tax

In 1427, the first income tax was called the *catasto* and was instituted by the Commune of Florence, Italy, for all the domains under Florentine rule. Proposed by Giovanni di Bicci de' Medici, a leader of the time, the tax was designed to bring about a more equal distribution of taxation. Each household was required to file a declaration of all assets, credits, and debts along with a list of its members. The information was used to calculate a taxable amount that was to be paid yearly.

Indoor Skating Rink

In 1862, the Victoria Skating Rink, the first indoor skating rink of notable record, opened in Montreal, Canada, as an ice rink. During the winter months, it was used for pleasure skating, ice hockey, and skating sports. During the summer, the ice was thawed and the building was used for musical performances and horticultural shows. The facility was a long, two-story brick building with a high-pitched roof supported from within by curving wooden trusses. Tall, round-arched windows ran the length of the building and illuminated the interior. Evening skating was made possible by 500 gas-jet lighting fixtures set in colored glass globes. Later in the rink's history, the lighting was converted to electric, making it the first building in Canada to be electrified. Another first for the Victoria: it housed the first indoor hockey game.

Indoor Toilet

King Minos of Crete had the first flushing water closet recorded in history more than 2,800 years ago … and that's about all that's known about it. Later, a crude toilet was discovered in the tomb of a Chinese king of the Western Han dynasty dating to anywhere from 206 B.C.E. to 24 C.E. Chamber pots, metal or ceramic bowls used and then emptied of the contents (many times out the window!), were used during the Middle Ages. In 1594, Sir John Harrington built a "prive in perfection" (flush toilet) for his godmother, Queen Elizabeth I of England. But it wasn't until 1775 that the first patent for the flushing toilet was issued to British watchmaker Alexander Cummings. With Cummings's design, the forerunner of the modern toilet, some water remained in the bowl after each flush.

Influenza Epidemic

1580 marked the first recorded widespread outbreak of the influenza virus as it swept across Asia Minor, northern Africa, and Europe, resulting in millions of deaths. The word *influenza* was derived from the Latin word *influentia*. Sixteenth-century Italians first applied the word *influenza* to outbreaks of any epidemic disease because they blamed such events on the influence of heavenly bodies. The 1580 flu outbreak was so wide-ranging that it was later labeled a pandemic, which is an epidemic over an extremely large area.

Inoculation

Although debatable, the earliest record of inoculation was found and practiced in eighth-century India for smallpox. Indian physician Madhav compiled a 79-chapter book called the *Nidāna* that listed diseases along with their causes, symptoms, and complications. Within the book, he included a special chapter on smallpox (*masūrikā*) that described a

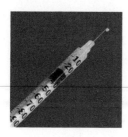

method of inoculation to protect against the disease. Treatment was done by pricking the skin of the patient's arm with a small metal instrument to inoculate with year-old smallpox matter that had been gathered from infected victims. The inoculators traveled all across India to administer the procedure.

Instant Camera

On February 21, 1947, the Land Camera was the first commercial
instant camera to be used. It had self-developing film and was invented
by American scientist Edwin Herbert Land, founder of the Polaroid
Corporation. The camera's specially prepared photographic paper had
pods of developer and a fixing agent sandwiched with the film. After
the snapshot was taken, the photographer turned a camera knob that
squeezed open one of the pods to develop the negative and make the
print. The completed picture was made in about 1 minute. The camera
was a hit.

Instant Coffee

The earliest, but unsubstantiated, version of instant coffee is said to have
appeared around 1771 in Britain. In 1901, the first successful technique
for manufacturing a stable powdered product was invented by Japanese
American chemist Satori Kato of Chicago. His just-add-hot-water
"instant" coffee used a process he had developed for making instant tea.
In 1906, English chemist George Constant Washington invented the
first mass-produced instant coffee. Living in Guatemala at the time,
Washington created and marketed "Red E Coffee" brand instant coffee
in 1909. In 1938, Nescafé invented its freeze-dried coffee.

Instant Creamer

In 1961, Glendale, California's Nestlé company produced Coffee-Mate,
the first powdered nondairy instant creamer. Coffee-Mate needed no
refrigeration, and half a spoonful or more could be added to black coffee
to whiten it and alter the coffee's taste. Before this time, coffee drinkers
had to add real dairy cream or milk. Coffee-Mate contained a milk
derivative with no lactose, corn syrup, or vegetable oil solids.

Instant Replay

In 1955, the Canadian Broadcasting Corporation (CBC), headquartered in Ottawa, Ontario, invented the first form of instant replay. It occurred when director George Retzlaff produced the first in-game replays that he used on *Hockey Night in Canada*, a sports show broadcast on Saturday evenings. Thanks to the instant replay, Retzlaff was able to show clips of scored goals within 30 seconds of the goal being made. He did this by employing a kinescope (the motion-picture record or film of a television program) that could be developed and replayed quickly, picking out the desired parts or action.

Insurance

Around 2000 B.C.E., the Babylonian traders practiced the first insurance, or early method of transferring or distributing risk. They were encouraged to assume the risks of the caravan trade through loans that were repaid with interest only after their goods had arrived safely at their destinations. If a merchant received a loan to fund his shipment, he would pay the lender an additional sum in exchange for the lender's guarantee to cancel the loan should the shipment be stolen or lost at sea. This procedure was given legal force in the Code of Hammurabi, a collection of the laws and edicts of the Babylonian king.

Intensive Care Unit

In 1854, the first intensive care unit (ICU) was the Monitoring Unit of critically wounded patients attended to under nurse Florence Nightingale's guidance. These units were in the British hospitals located in Constantinople (now Istanbul, Turkey) during the Crimean War. Nightingale led more than three dozen nurses to section off the gravest of patients for more attentive care; before this, the mortality rate of hospitalized soldiers was as high as 40 percent. Nightingale instigated a "critical care protocol" of separating patients by severity of injuries and illnesses so they could receive more medical care. This practice made the mortality rate fall to 2 percent and paved the way for future ICUs.

Internet Domain

On March 15, 1985, Symbolics.com became the first registered Internet domain. Researchers at the University of Wisconsin had just introduced the Internet domain name system (DNS) with ordinary words as names in 1984. With the name server, users were no longer required to remember lengthy numbers to know the exact path to other systems. From their connected computers, users could type in a name or series of letters to get to a website. Symbolics, a computer manufacturing company, was bankrupt by the early 1990s, but the first registered Internet domain lives on with new owners.

Interstate Highway

Commissioned on March 29, 1806, the National Road was the first federally financed interstate. Running from Cumberland, Maryland, through Pennsylvania, West Virginia, Ohio, and Indiana, to Vandalia, Illinois, it took decades to finish. The approximate 700 miles of what was initially little more than a dirt road helped open the land west of the Appalachians to settlers and commerce. Later paved and lengthened to span its 824-mile route, the National Road eventually evolved into US 40. It was the first official road linking multiple states.

Jet

In October 1910, the Coanda-1910 made its first and only flight. It was the world's first air reactive (jet) airplane, invented by Henri Coanda of Bucharest, Romania. The jet had no propeller, and its wings were made with steel leading edges instead of wood. The gasoline engine's layout was the real innovation: it was housed under a cowl and through a gearbox, and turned a compressor at 4,000 rotations per minute. The engine's combustion-thrust was much greater than that of a normal gasoline engine and propeller. It was created by mixing the compressor's exhaust, the gasoline engine's exhaust, and additional fuel. This mixture was ported into two ring-shape burning chambers located on each side of the fuselage.

Jigsaw Puzzle

Around 1760, John Spilsbury, a London engraver and mapmaker, introduced the first jigsaw puzzle in England. The puzzle was a map of England and surrounding countries. Each piece of the puzzle was a sepa-

rate country. There were no interlocking pieces, but rather the pieces simply butted up to each other. To produce the puzzle, Spilsbury glued one of his maps to a thin sheet of hardwood. He then cut out around the national boundaries using a fine-bladed saw. For the finishing touches, he added some hand painting and applied a veneer finish. The end product was soon used as an educational aid to teach geography to British children in a fun way.

Jukebox

On November 23, 1889, the forerunner to the modern jukebox was the Nickel-in-the-Slot machine, a coin-operated phonograph player placed in the Palais Royale Saloon in San Francisco, California, by Louis Glass and William Arnold. This first jukebox was a modified Edison Class M electric phonograph. It was housed in an oak cabinet refitted with a coin mechanism patented by Glass and Arnold. There was no amplification, and patrons had to listen to whatever music was on the queue using one of four listening tubes. The device was highly successful and earned more than $1,000 in its first 6 months.

King

Around 2333 B.C.E., Tangun Wanggom established the first acknowledged kingdom in what is now Korea and served as both king and shaman. (*Tangun* means "god of the earth," *wang* means "king," and *gom* represents "priest" or "shaman.") The world's first king was an enterprising ruler who was loved and seemingly worshipped by his followers.

Tangun called his land Choson and is credited with inaugurating a national religion and establishing a national capital at Asadal (now Pyongyang, North Korea). Although some dismiss King Tangun as only a legend, Chinese records written 20 to 30 centuries before Christ do mention the land of Choson.

Kite

Around 400 B.C.E., the first kites were called *Muyuan*. These early Chinese kites were made of lightweight woods for support and structure and had thin wooden sheets as facings and walls. The first kites were aerodynamic, relatively large, and had the power to lift several pounds. They were held together by twined knots and natural epoxy resins and were flown and guided while attached to cords or flexible wooden rods. Hand-painted designs and scenes were common decorations. The kites were used for many varied purposes such as communicating with the gods, divination, funerals, distractions to enemies, and even for fishing.

Laptop Computer

In 1968, the first concept of a laptop computer was the Dynabook, created by Alan Kay of the Xerox Palo Alto Research Center in California. Kay's vision was a notebook-size wireless portable computer actually for children more than for adults. The Dynabook never got past sketches and a cardboard model, but in 1972, Kay's ideas did lead to the development of the Xerox Alto prototype. It was called the Interim Dynabook, but

the project never went much further except to set the tone for the development of a truly portable laptop computer in the future.

Introduced in 1982, the GRiD Compass 1100 was likely the first commercial computer created in a laptop format and one of the first truly portable machines.

Laser Beam

On July 7, 1960, Theodore Harold Maiman, a Hughes Aircraft Company researcher in Malibu, California, first demonstrated the working laser beam in public. Maiman's ruby laser was the first successful optical or light laser. It was based on the evolving works of Charles Townes and Arthur Schawlow who, in 1954, had invented the "maser" (microwave amplification by stimulated emission of radiation) using ammonia gas and microwave radiation. *Laser* is an acronym for "light amplification by the stimulated emission of radiation."

Latex Glove

In 1894, 5 years after Johns Hopkins Hospital opened in Baltimore, Maryland, William Stewart Halsted, the hospital's first surgeon-in-chief, developed and introduced the first rubber surgical gloves. Although Halsted may not have invented the surgical glove, he introduced the sterile latex reusable glove into the operating room after he realized latex was an effective substance to provide a barrier to prevent infections. Many consider Halsted "the father of the surgical glove."

Laundromat

On April 18, 1934, J. F. Cantrell opened the first Laundromat in Fort Worth, Texas. Cantrell noticed that personal washing machines were a luxury many of his neighbors simply could not afford, so he got a great idea and filled a needed niche. His first Laundromat, which he called Washateria, had four electric washing machines but no dryers. The washers were not coin-operated; Cantrell charged by the hour for the use of each machine. Patrons brought their own soap.

Lawnmower

Edwin Beard Budding, a textile engineer from Stroud, Gloucestershire, England, invented the first lawnmower in 1830. It was a mechanical push-type mower made of cast iron and featured gear wheels that transmitted power from the rear roller to the cutting cylinder. Budding based his idea on a device used for trimming the nap on cloth, but he had to figure out how the mechanism could be mounted in a wheeled frame to make the blades rotate close to a lawn's surface. He did, and his concept worked. Budding patented the idea and went into a production partnership with another local engineer, John Ferrabee of Phoenix Iron Works.

Lethal Injection

In October 1939, unscrupulous physicians in Nazi Germany conducted the first lethal injections, working under a program called Action T4 that eventually caused the deaths of about 275,000 innocent people. The physicians were exterminating patients under direction of Adolf Hitler's secret memo of September 1, 1939, indicating that suffering patients "judged incurably sick, by critical medical examination that may appear incurable" should be killed with a liquid mixture of psychoactive drugs, mainly sedatives from the barbiturates family. Action T4 was later replaced with poison gas showers.

On December 7, 1982, Charles "Charlie" Brooks Jr. of Fort Worth, Texas, was the first convict to be killed by lethal injection after being injected with sodium pentathol.

Lie Detector

The first mention of a method for detecting lies was by British novelist Daniel DeFoe in a 1730 essay he wrote titled "An Effectual Scheme for the Immediate Preventing of Street Robberies and Suppressing All Other Disorders of the Night." He suggested that taking the pulse of a suspicious fellow was a practical and humane method of identifying a criminal because a fast pulse indicated suspicion of guilt. DeFoe's was the earliest suggestion of a method to employ medical science in the fight against crime.

Lighthouse

Around 285 B.C.E., the people of the Pharos peninsula in Alexandria, Egypt, marked the harbor, creating the world's first marine lighthouse. The project, later hailed as one of the Seven Wonders of the World, was engineered by Sostratus of Cnidus. The 350-foot-high lighthouse took many years to build and was constructed in three stages: square, octagonal, and circular. Access to its entrance was up a long, vaulted ramp. A spiral staircase led up to the many chambers that provided pathways to the third story, where a fire burned on the summit. This first lighthouse stood until the mid-fourteenth century, when it was destroyed by an earthquake.

Lightning Rod

Around 1730, the Leaning Tower of Nevyansk in Sverdlovsk Oblast, Russia, was topped with the first lightning rod. Russian architects devised it along with the tower's other advanced technologies. The roof of the tower was crowned with a metallic rod in the shape of a pointed gilded sphere with spikes. Several wired cables ran from the rod down the sides of the tower into the ground. This successfully protected the tower by taking lightning strikes away from the structure and into the ground.

Limb Reattachment

On May 23, 1962, Dr. Ronald A. Malt, a Boston, Massachusetts, surgeon, along with a team of 12 specialists, oversaw the first successful reattachment of a human limb, the right arm of 12-year-old Everett Knowles. The youngster had been hopping a freight train to go to a baseball game and was thrown against a stone abutment, which caused his arm to be ripped off cleanly at the shoulder. The surgery was conducted at the Massachusetts General Hospital, and a year later, the boy was able to move all five fingers and bend his wrist. Two years afterward, he was playing baseball and tennis. *Life* magazine called it "the most celebrated arm in all the world."

Liquid Soap

William Sheppard of New York City patented liquid soap on August 22, 1865. Patent number 49561 depicted his discovery "that by the addition of comparatively small quantities of common soap to a large quantity of spirits of ammonia or hartshorn is thickened to the consistency of molasses, and a liquid soap is obtained of superior detergent qualities." Sheppard dissolved the soap in liquid form in water or by steam to the consistency of molasses. Then he mixed 1 pound of regular soap with 100 pounds of spirits of hartshorn (the ammoniacal liquor resulting from distilling horn shavings). This first liquid soap soon became useful for both domestic and manufacturing purposes.

Literary Agent

The first literary agent, someone who acts on the behalf of a client, was Alexander Pollock Watt, of Aberdeen, Scotland. In 1875, Watt established A. P. Watt and Company, Limited, the world's first literary agency, after a friend asked him to negotiate a contract with a London publishing company. Watt defined and set the standard for the role of the literary agent, developing strong friendships with the authors he represented. His son, A. S. Watt, took over the literary agency after his father's death in 1914. The agency, which is still operating and headquartered in London today, attracted many important authors, among them Pearl Buck, W. Somerset Maugham, Mark Twain, William Butler Keats, Herbert George Wells, Rudyard Kipling, Wilkie Collins, Arthur Conan Doyle, G. K. Chesterton, and others.

Little League

In 1939, Carl E. Stotz of Williamsport, Pennsylvania, founded Little League Baseball. The first game was played on a vacant lot after Stotz enlisted help from others in his community. Three teams of boys under age 13 were formed—Lundy Lumber, Lycoming Dairy, and Jumbo Pretzel. A $30 donation was sufficient to purchase uniforms for each of the three teams whose managers were Stotz, George Bebble, and Bert Bebble. In that first-ever Little League game, Lundy Lumber defeated Lycoming Dairy 23–8, but Lycoming Dairy came back to win the season's first-half title. They faced second-half champ Lundy Lumber in a best-of-three series. Lycoming Dairy won the final game of the series by the score of 3–2.

Log Cabin

The first log cabin dates to long, long ago. The technique of building with horizontally laid logs joined at the corners with specially carved notches is an old European tradition brought to the New World in the 1600s. Swedish immigrants constructed America's first log cabins in 1638 when they built the town of New Sweden (near present-day Trenton, New Jersey). These early cabins were small, one-room buildings that measured 12x14 feet or so that housed an entire family. They usually had a fireplace at one end and sleeping quarters in a loft.

Lottery

Aside from biblical references to drawing lots, the first public lottery of note with cash prizes took place in 1530 in Florence, Italy. Called *La Lotto de Firenze*, this game of chance was a number lottery that awarded money to its winners. The concept was the expanded idea of a 1515 custom in Genoa, Italy, in which names were randomly drawn for election to the Senate. For the 1530 notion, the names were changed to plain numbers. The word *lottery* is derived from the Italian word *lotto*, meaning "destiny" or "fate."

Loudspeaker

On April 14, 1874, the first loudspeaker was described in a U.S. patent by Ernst W. Siemens of Berlin, Germany. His improved magneto-electric induction apparatus, in which a magnet excites electric currents, applied the mechanical movement of an electrical coil from the electrical currents transmitted through it. However, initially he did not use the device for audible magnification transmissions. After making some adaptations, he was later granted German and British patents for his sound radiator of a moving-coil transducer with a flaring morning glory (flowerlike) trumpet form. Siemens's device later became the loudspeaker horn used on most phonographs players.

Mail-Order Business

In 1744, American Benjamin Franklin produced and printed the first mail-order catalog to sell scientific and academic books. The catalog also came with the first mail-order guarantee: "Those persons who live remote, by sending their orders and money to B. Franklin (in Philadelphia) may depend on the same justice as if present." In 2004, Franklin was inducted into the Direct Marketing Association's Hall of Fame.

Margarine

In 1870, Hippolyte Mège-Mouriez from Provence, France, created margarine in response to a request by Emperor Louis Napoleon III for a satisfactory butter substitute. Mège-Mouriez used margaric acid, a fatty acid component isolated in 1813 by Michael Chevreul and named because of the lustrous pearly drops that reminded Chevreul of the Greek word for pearl, *margarites*. From this word, Mège-Mouriez coined the name *margarine* for his invention, the invention that later claimed the emperor's prize.

Matchbook

The first paper matchbook folder, called Flexibles, was patented in September 1882 by Philadelphia, Pennsylvania, patent attorney Joshua Pusey. Pusey had become frustrated with carrying around bulky boxes of wooden matches to keep lighting his cigars, so he created a device made up of lighter, smaller paper matches that were secured to a thin paper wrapping with an attached striking surface. This first matchbook contained 50 paper matches and positioned the striking surface on the inside of the paper fold. In 1896, Pusey sold his invention to the Diamond Match Company for $4,000.

Maternity Clothes

In 1660 in France, during the Baroque Period and onward, the Adrienne was a gownlike garment with no waist and lots of voluminous folds to cover a growing body, specifically a pregnant body. It fit loosely, but it did try to follow the shape of the female figure. Previously in history, there was no need for specialized maternity wear because all dresses were big and loose-fitting. The French-fashioned Adrienne took over the leading role for maternity fashion in Europe, and the rest of world followed.

Medical School

In the ninth century, Almum et Hippocraticum Medicorum Collegium, located in Salerno, near Naples in southern Italy, became the first modern medical school. Although founded in the ninth century, it was formally organized in the tenth century and reached its peak at the end of the twelfth century. The most famous teacher at the school was Constantine Africanus from Carthage, North Africa, who taught there in the eleventh century. For students to earn licensure, they had to work through 3 years of college work, 4 years of medical study, 1 year of practice with a physician, and another year of anatomy for surgery. The Salerno school is still in operation today.

Microchip

In the late 1940s and early 1950s, British electronic author Geoffrey William Arnold Dummer was the first to conceptualize the integrated circuit, commonly called the microchip. His electronic work findings stated the possibility to fabricate multiple circuit elements on and into a substance like silicon. In 1952, he presented his discoveries at a conference in Washington, D.C. This was some 6 years before Jack Kirby of Texas Instruments was awarded a patent for basically the same idea. History calls Dummer "the prophet of the integrated circuit."

Microwave Oven

In 1946, Dr. Percy Spencer of the Raytheon Corporation in Waltham, Massachusetts, accidentally discovered the effects of the microwaves on food. While testing a new vacuum tube called a magnetron, he observed that the candy bar in his pocket had melted. The surrounding microwaves had cooked the candy bar and nothing else. The Raytheon Corporation produced the first commercial microwave oven in 1954, and Amana, a division of Raytheon, produced the first domestic version in 1967. Today, more than 90 percent of American homes have a microwave oven. LG Electronics of Seoul, Korea, is the number one global manufacturer.

Military School

During the eighth century in ancient Greece, the first military schools were established in the city-state of Sparta. After fighting two wars with the neighboring state of Messina, Sparta transformed its city-state into a military society. To survive during that time, Sparta dictated that all schools be military schools and the principle purpose of all education was the development of soldiers. Boys were sent to a residential military school at age 6 or 7 and continued until they were 18 to 20 years of age. They were subject to rigorous testing, and if they failed, they were not considered citizens and received no political rights.

Milk Carton

The U.S. Patent Office granted toy factory owner John Van Wormer of Toledo, Ohio, a patent for his "paper bottle" on October 19, 1915.

He got the idea after accidentally dropping a glass milk bottle one morning, which undoubtedly made a mess. Van Wormer called his new product Pure-Pak, and marketed the idea that it could be thrown away after one use, eliminating the need to return glass milk bottles. The concept didn't catch on quickly, as Americans were very attached to milk in bottles, but a steady increase in glass costs worked in Van Wormer's favor. Soon other companies started making their own paper milk cartons, and by 1950 Van Wormer was churning out 20 million a

day. A tab on the side of the gable was created to make pouring possible. This opening device was primitive by today's standards; it wasn't until the mid-1950s that the current spout was introduced. By 1968, more than 70 percent of milk packaged in the United States went into paper gable-top milk cartons.

Minimum Wage

Although New Zealand and Australia set up labor arbitration boards in the 1890s, the United States instigated the first national minimum wage on October 24, 1938, at 25¢ per hour. The Fair Labor Standards Act (FLSA) set the lowest wage at which workers could sell their labor. The FLSA also guaranteed time and a half for overtime in certain jobs and prohibited most employment of minors in oppressive child labor.

Miniskirt

In 1964, French fashion designer Andre Courrèges invented the first miniskirt, and soon his creation was copied over and over around the world. With the help of his "ascetic scissors," Courrèges turned out garments that were magical in their simplicity and appealed to a younger, hipper generation. His miniskirt elongated the leg and was the shortest in Paris. Its cool colors were offered in pink, white, ice-blue, pale turquoise, day-glow orange, and lime green. Courrèges's "space-age" miniskirt was a square-shape skirt that fell several inches above the knee and was suggested to be pleasantly accompanied by calf-high boots.

Miracle in the Bible

The first miracle in the Bible was creation, as found in the Book of Genesis starting with verse 1: "In the beginning God created the heaven and the earth." (King James Version) Much later, around 27 C.E., Jesus performed his first miracle, the turning of water into wine at a wedding feast. This miracle is accounted in the Book of John 2:1–11.

Miss America

On September 8, 1921, 16-year-old Margaret Gorman of Washington, D.C., was crowned the winner in what was to become the first Miss America pageant. The gala took place in Atlantic City, New Jersey, and as contestants were being selected, Herb Test, a local newspaperman, enthusiastically proclaimed, "And we'll call her Miss America!" On capturing the title, Miss Gorman was awarded the Golden Mermaid trophy and $100. She was chosen from only a handful of contestants by an equal combination of the crowd's applause as the contestants strutted in swimsuits and points given to her by a panel of judges. Standing 5'1" tall and weighing 108 pounds, Miss Gorman's bust, waist, and hip measurements were 30-25-32. Upon winning, she was crowned, wrapped in an American flag, and paraded around as Miss America. This first Miss America also bore a striking resemblance to Mary Pickford, the popular screen actress of the era.

Missile

Around 1000 C.E., the Chinese invented missile rockets as a spin-off from their gunpowder invention. The Chinese military engineers invented hollow bamboo tubes packed with powder and fixed to incendiary arrows. To aim the missile or set its projected path, they adjusted the angle of the rocket before launch. These first missiles added a new dimension to fireworks but inevitably were applied to warfare, as they were able to set enemy cities on fire from a distance.

Mobile Home

Throughout Europe in the 1400s, the first mobile homes of note were the gypsy wagons. The gypsies traveled in roaming bands with their horse-drawn living wagons, or mobile homes. Each home was equipped with a bed, stove, closet, and several chests. Part of it was carpeted and partitioned off to accommodate a sleeping place. Curtains shaded its windows. A portion of the home served as a kitchen and was fitted with a stove whose small chimney passed up through the roof. The closet held a great pitcher of water, a few cooking utensils, and extra supplies and clothes. Portions of the wagon's exterior were where the lady of the home could place ornaments, decorations, and usually some well-thumbed tambourines.

Money

Around 9000 B.C.E., the first concept of money was instigated, but not in the traditional sense. Instead of coins, shells, or other small trinkets, cattle were used as money. By definition, money is any circulating medium of exchange used to buy or to get things. The barter process was the exchange of things of value that one has for other goods that are wanted, a trading of this for that. Livestock were often used as a unit of exchange. Then as agriculture developed, people used crops such as grain for bartering.

Money Order

The money order system was first formally established in Great Britain in 1792 by a private company, not a bank or postal entity. A money order is a payment order for a specified amount of money and is paid for in advance. The first money orders were difficult to process and had fees on both ends. They were proportionally expensive and not very successful. When the system started in England, it was supposed to somehow help one to save money. The people did not accept the idea until the mid-1830s, when the system was taken over by the post office.

Monopoly

Around 1878 B.C.E., ancient Egypt had the first monopoly, which was on grain because of a 7-year famine. The monopoly came about because the pharaoh had experienced prophetic dreams that Joseph interpreted to foretell a famine. Joseph recommended that Egypt make preparations by stockpiling great amounts of food. The pharaoh then instituted a system for storing and rationing grain to see Egypt through the long, hard years. The monopoly stretched farther than Egypt, as accounted in Genesis 41:57: "And all countries came into Egypt to Joseph for to buy corn; because the famine was so sore (severe) in all lands." (King James Version)

Mosque

Built more than 2,000 years ago, the first mosque was the Kaaba, and/or the area nearby. The prophet Abraham built the Kaaba as a shrine for the House of God. Located in Mecca, Saudi Arabia, the Kaaba is a cube-shape stone structure located inside the courtyard of the building, also a mosque, constructed around it. This building, still in existence, has immense indoor and outdoor praying spaces. It's officially called the Sacred Mosque of Mecca, Al Masjid Al-Haram, but it's more commonly known as the Haram or Haram Sharif. When Muslims all across the world pray, this first mosque is the direction they face.

Motel

The Milestone Mo-Tel (later the Motel Inn) opened its doors in San Luis Obispo, California, on December 12, 1925. Developed by architect

Arthur S. Heineman of Pasadena, California, the Milestone cost $80,000 to build. Heineman wanted to create a "motor hotel" with characteristics between rustic auto camps and conventional hotels. Heineman found that the words *motor hotel* didn't fit on his sign, so he scrunched them together to make *motel*. Favoring a Spanish mission, the Milestone had dozens of bungalows and accommodations for 160 guests. It offered easy access to the highway, reasonable prices, privacy, and a little anonymity. For $1.25 a night, paying guests got a two-room bungalow with a kitchen, bathroom, and private adjoining garage.

Motorcycle

Around 1867, the first motorcycle was a steam-powered American invention built by Sylvester Howard Roper of Roxbury, Massachusetts, who demonstrated it at fairs and circuses. The charcoal-fired, two-cylinder engine was on a specially built chassis. A vertical boiler was suspended between two 34-inch-diameter wooden-spoke wheels. Charcoal was fed through a small circular door on the side of the firebox. The motorcycle had a throttle on the handlebar, footrests, and a friction brake. Although the Roper steam motorcycle wasn't commercially successful, the two-wheeled velocipede was road tested.

Mouthwash

The first known reference to mouth rinsing appeared around 2700 B.C.E. in the Chinese treatment of gum disease that recommended rinsing the mouth with urine. The modern era of mouthwash began in 1914 when Listerine became the first commercially available mouthwash sold over the counter. (Since 1895, it had been sold to dental professionals only as a powerful oral antiseptic.) A new advertising campaign marketed the product as a remedy for bad breath and introduced the American public to the term *halitosis* and its social undesirability.

Movie

On June 11, 1878, the first motion picture, or movie, was shot before the press and starred a horse named Sallie Gardner at a Palo Alto, California, farm. The sponsors of the movie, Leland Stanford (later founder of Stanford University) and Eadweard Muybridge (inventor of a new photographic technology), wanted to establish whether a galloping horse ever has all four feet off the ground simultaneously. To experiment, the horse was photographed in fast motion using a series of 24 stereo-scopic cameras. The galloping motion was illustrated through a series of still images viewed together. This first movie proved that a galloping horse does experience all four feet off the ground at the same time.

Movie Actor

The actors of the first silent movies were not credited as they are today because in addition to acting, they were the stagehands and set decora-tors as well. In 1903, American actor Max Aronson (a.k.a. Bronco Billy, Max Anderson, and Gilbert M. Anderson) made his first movie appear-ance in *The Great Train Robbery*. As the first movie actor, Aronson played three roles in the movie: the bandit, the brakeman, and the passenger who was shot. Besides acting, Aronson also wrote and directed, and he later became the first cowboy star.

Movie Actress

During the early days of silent movies, the names of the actresses were not publicized as they are today. In 1906, at 20 years of age, Canadian-born Florence Lawrence made her first motion picture and is often cred-ited as the first movie star. Her acting talents guided her to also become known as the biograph girl, the imp girl, and the girl of a thousand faces. Throughout her acting career, Lawrence appeared in more than 270 films for various motion picture companies.

Movie Festival

On August 6, 1932, the world's first major film festival was held in Venice, Italy. The first festival wasn't competitive; therefore, no prize was awarded. That didn't come until the second festival, when the Golden Lion was awarded for the best film. During the first festival, the sole film shown was *Dr. Jekyll and Mr. Hyde*, directed by Ruben Mamoulian. The movie was a screen adaptation of Robert Louis Stevenson's 1886 novel. The festival still takes place today as the Venice Cinema Art Festival.

Movie Kiss

The first movie kiss (and calling it a "movie" is a bit of a stretch as it was more of a short film clip) was in an 1896 clip titled *The Kiss*, also called *The Widow Jones*. In the silent film created by Thomas Edison, the first known kiss caught on film was a 47-second re-creation of a stage kiss from the musical *The Widow Jones*. The couple involved were John C. Rice and May Irwin. The clip was considered scandalous at the time, but history marks it as one of the most memorable early films.

Movie Musical

The first movie musical was 1929's *The Broadway Melody*. Billed as Metro-Goldwyn-Mayer's "All Talking All Singing All Dancing" picture, it was a smash hit and won the Academy Award for Best Picture. The musical was written by Norman Houston and James Gleason; directed by Harry Beaumont; and starred Charles King, Anita Page, and Bessie Love. The plot follows the romances of musical comedy stars set against the backstage of a Broadway revue. Other firsts for *The Broadway Melody*: it became the first sound movie to win Best Picture, and composer George Cohan's "Give My Regards to Broadway" was given its talkie debut in the film.

Movie Rating

Aside from local city boards who tried to censor or rate movies, it was on October 7, 1968, when the movie industry adopted a universal film ratings system for the first time. Prior to that, filmmakers followed the self-imposed Motion Picture Production Code of 1930, commonly called the Hays Code. The first movie ratings in 1968 were G for general audiences, M for mature audiences, R for no one under 16 admitted without an adult, and X for no one under 16 admitted. This first ratings system removed the restriction regarding what type of content could be included in films and gave moviegoers the information necessary to determine if a certain film contained content they wanted to view or allow their children to see.

Movie Theater

On June 26, 1896, the first movie theater to run shows on a regular basis was Vitascope Hall in New Orleans, Louisiana. There was no concession stand, smoking was permitted, and tickets cost 10¢ each, which allowed moviegoers to sit in available seats on a first-come-first-served basis. The theater seated 400 viewers and was the brainchild of the English-born William T. "Pop" Rock, a pioneering film exhibitor who used vigorous advertising slogans that included "After Breakfast Visit the Vitascope." Rock also instigated coupons that admitted any child under the age of 10 for free if accompanied by an adult. The first viewings were short movies of comic pieces and scenic landscapes. The venture proved to be profitable.

MRI

On July 3, 1977, the first human magnetic resonance image (MRI) was made of the chest cavity of Dr. Lawrence Minkoff in the Downstate Medical Center in Brooklyn, New York. The MRI machine, named

Indomitable, took 4 hours, 45 minutes to produce an image. Dr. Raymond Damadian, an American physician and researcher, along with post-graduate assistants Doctors Larry Minkoff and Michael Goldsmith, had worked for several years to reach this point. This first scanner was conceived to take advantage of the relaxation differences among the body's tissues. It provided imaging contrast that was many times better than that of x-rays.

Municipal Bus Service

In March 1662, Blaise Pascal, a French innovator, physicist, and math-ematician, devised the concept of, secured financing for, and launched operations for the first municipal bus service. The horse-drawn omni-buses were to "circulate along a predetermined route in Paris at regular intervals regardless of the number of passengers." Pascal's bus service started with 7 horse-drawn vehicles, each able to carry 6 to 8 passengers. Initially, it was a free service, but when a fare was introduced, ridership declined. The bus routes were out of business by 1675. Also contributing to their demise was the fact that France was in tough economic times.

Murder in the Bible

The first murder in the Bible occurred when Cain, a farmer, killed his brother Abel, a shepherd, in the creation year 36. The two were the first and second sons of Adam and Eve. According to Genesis 4:1–16, Cain killed his brother after God rejected Cain's sacrifice but accepted Abel's. Cain's sacrifice was fruits of the soil, while Abel's was fat portions of flock. Genesis 4:8 further explains: "And Cain talked with Abel his brother: and it came to pass, when they were in the field, that Cain rose up against Abel his brother, and slew him." (King James Version) It was premeditated murder caused by anger, jealousy, and pride.

Music Video

The modern music video has its roots in the first Beatles major motion picture, *A Hard Day's Night*. Throughout the 1964 movie, there were musical segments of songs. The first music video was in the movie's opening credits song, "A Hard Day's Night," which showed fans chasing The Beatles. The next song, "I Should Have Known Better," portrayed The Beatles actually singing the song and playing musical instruments. Also in 1964, the band began filming short promotional films, or music videos, for their songs to be aired on television variety shows. They were clips from the movie.

National Flag

On June 14, 1777, the first national flag was the American flag, which represented the United States of America. The flag symbolized a country status and was formally adopted as the national standard by the  Second Continental Congress. Except for the adding of a new star for each new state that joined the union and changes in the arrangement of the stars, the flag displayed today is the same as the first flag. Legend has it that a group headed by George Washington commissioned seamstress Betsy Ross to implement their design for presentation to Congress.

National Holiday

The first national holiday, the Centennial Celebration of Washington's Inaugural, was held April 30, 1889, as authorized by an act of Congress on March 21, 1889, in observance of the centennial of the inauguration of President George Washington. Various societies, large and small, all across the United States held parades and inaugural balls to honor the former president. Although no longer a national holiday, the Centennial Celebration of Washington's Inaugural set the stage for considerations for other noteworthy events to be honored.

National Park

On March 1, 1872, President Ulysses S. Grant signed into law an act of Congress that established Yellowstone National Park as the first lands to be set aside for public use, which made Yellowstone the world's first national park. The park, administered by the federal government "for the benefit and enjoyment of the people," was a tract of land 55 by 65 miles, located about the sources of the Yellowstone and Missouri Rivers in present-day Wyoming, Montana, and Idaho. George Catlin, a self-taught artist, is generally credited with conceptualizing a national park.

Neon Sign

In 1912, the first commercial neon sign was sold to a Paris barber. Its 3½-foot-tall red letters spelled out CINZANO, which probably referred to the manufacturer of several famous Italian products, including wines. Paris-born chemist and inventor George Claude's associate, Jaques Fonseque, sold the sign. Earlier, Claude had discovered that passing an electric current through inert gases made them light up very brightly. In 1910, Claude made his first public display of neon lamp, lighting two 38-foot-long tubes at the Paris Expo.

News Agency

During the sixteenth century in what is now modern Italy, the first news agency was a private group of correspondents paid by the merchants and traders of Venice to collect and deliver information, especially on the movements of the Ottoman Turkish fleet, which was in a conquering, looting mode. It was, at times, very dangerous work as the correspondents pooled their efforts and news-gathering sources. The news agency reported on anything that might affect the shipping and commerce trades, such as the safest trade routes and cargo manifests. Although most of the reported news was verbally dispersed, some centralized written letters were distributed.

News Correspondent

From his earliest days in radio broadcasting in 1932 to his last *All Things Considered* commentary in 2000, Robert Trout was the first news correspondent of note. Born Robert Albert Blondheim in 1909 Wake County, North Carolina, his career spanned virtually the entire history of radio news, including the repeal of Prohibition, the coverage of World War II, and numerous presidential elections and coronations. Trout coined the phrase "fireside chat" to describe President Franklin Delano Roosevelt's radio addresses. In March 1938, he conducted the first CBS *World News Roundup* that presented on-the-spot reporting via shortwave from reporters all over Europe. Trout's accomplishments go on and on. He died in November 2000 at the age of 92, 2 weeks after his final National Public Radio broadcast.

Newspaper

The first known forms of regularly distributed written information were the newspapers or news posters published in Rome around 59 B.C.E. These first newspapers were parchment sheets called *Acta Diurna Populi Romani* (*Daily Transactions of the Roman People*) and *Acta Senatus* (*Transactions of the Senate*). They kept the public informed about current events, including conflicts, governmental affairs, executions, deaths, births, and marriages. The text was handwritten multiple times and posted on buildings around Rome and other cities. It was then recopied by scribes to be further hand distributed. One of Julius Caesar's first acts of power was to require the *Acta* to be published on a daily basis.

Newsreel

Introduced in July 1906, the first newsreel was *London Day by Day*, produced by British filmmaker Will G. Barker. The newsreel was a short, silent documentary regularly released in a public presentation place and contained filmed news stories and items of topical interest. *London*

Day by Day featured daily events of London street life and was shown at the Empire Theater in Leicester Square. This daily first newsreel was short-lived due to the tremendous workload and expense required to continually produce and distribute it. Newspapers still provided the best news at that time.

Nuclear Power Plant

On June 27, 1954, the USSR's Obninsk Nuclear Power Plant went online. Constructed by Soviet engineers and located about 55 miles from Moscow, it was the world's first nuclear power plant to generate electricity for a power grid. Its output was around 5 megawatts of electric power, which was enough to power about 2,000 then-modern homes. It was also the first nuclear power station in the world. The Obninsk plant was a prototype design that used a graphite moderator and water coolant and was a forerunner for future designs and nuclear developments. It ceased operations April 29, 2002, due to lack of funding and loss of popularity for nuclear power.

Nuclear-Powered Ship

The world's first nuclear-powered vessel, the USS *Nautilus* (SSN 571), was christened on January 21, 1954. The U.S. Navy submarine was planned and personally supervised by Admiral Hyman G. Rickover, "the father of the nuclear navy." After various tests, the vessel was put to sea on January 17, 1955, and signaled her historic message: "Underway 11:00 on nuclear power." The *Nautilus* measured 320 feet in length and carried 13 officers and 92 enlisted men. In addition to being the first nuclear-powered ship, it also holds the title of the first submerged voyage under the North Pole. The *Nautilus* was used in the naval blockade of Cuba during the 1962 Cuban Missile Crisis. The sub's last voyage under its own power was in 1979, and on May 20, 1982, it was designated a National Historic Landmark. Today, the USS *Nautilus* is part of the U.S. Navy Submarine Force Museum in Groton, Connecticut.

Nursing School

Around 250 B.C.E., the first nursing school was started in India, founded by the works of the great physician Charaka. No women were allowed as students because only men were considered "pure" enough to become nurses. The policy of the *Charaka Samhita*, a document written by Charaka, stated that these men "should be imbued with kindness, competent to cook food, skilled in bathing and washing the patient, rubbing and massaging the limbs, lifting and assisting him to walk about, well skilled in making and cleansing of beds, and never unwilling to do anything that may be ordered." Charaka was also the first physician to present the concepts of digestion, metabolism, and immunity.

Observatory

From around 300 B.C.E., the Thirteen Towers of Chankillo constituted an ancient sun observatory. Located in Peru within an area of rock outcrops and sand ramps, the observatory consists of a 1,000-foot-long spread of cubic stone blocks that are regularly spaced apart, forming a toothed horizon. About 750 feet to the east and west are two observation points. From these vantage points, the towers along the horizon correspond to the rising and setting positions of the sun over the course of a year. This first observatory was also used to mark solar dates.

Ocean Oil Spill

Aside from the spillage aftermath of military oil tankers sunk during the strategic warfare of World War II, the first oil spill from a commercial tanker of note occurred March 18, 1967. The supertanker *Torrey Canyon* ran aground off the coast of Cornwall, England, and struck Pollard's Rock in the Seven Stone Reef. The 974-foot tanker spilled some 119,000 tons of Kuwaiti crude oil into the sea, creating an oil slick that was 35 miles long and almost 20 miles wide. The vessel was under the command of Italian-born Captain Pastrengo Rugiati. Apparently, strong currents pushed the ship off course while it was on autopilot.

Oil Strike

On August 27, 1859, Titusville, Pennsylvania, became the birthplace of the oil industry. It was there that the first commercial oil well in the world was drilled and the first oil strike took place. Former railroad conductor Edwin L. Drake, working for the Seneca Oil Company at the time, opened a 70-foot shaft by using an old steam engine to power the drill. Drake struck oil at 69½ feet but had been prepared to drill 1,000 feet if necessary. Before this oil strike, Drake was the subject of much ridicule. Others laughed at his theory that drilling would be the best way to extract oil from the earth. During its heyday, the Titusville oil well produced some 400 gallons a day.

Online Dating Service

From the late 1980s to the early 1990s, the predecessor of Internet dating was soc.singles, followed closely by alt.romance. Both were newsgroups with a massive collection of articles filled with questions, answers, views, and ideas on all things concerning romance and love. These newsgroups were a place to hang out, debate issues, and of course flirt. People from around the world logged on to these first online matchup sites to unwind, have fun, and maybe "meet" someone worthwhile.

Opera

Written and performed in 1597, the first opera (known by that name) was *Dafne*. Its libretto was written by poet Ottavio Rinuccini, and its music was by Florentine choirmaster Jacopo Peri. First performed in Florence, Italy, *Dafne* was commissioned by the Count of Vernio. Its storyline was a version of the Greek myth of Daphne and Apollo and was a collection of recitatives separated by occasional orchestral interludes. The word *opera* was invented by a group of late Renaissance Italian intellectuals to describe their new artistic form that combined music, drama, scenery, and movement. It means "a work" or "labor."

Origami

Paper folding originated in China around the first or second century C.E. for the purpose of folding certain special documents such as certificates  and diplomas. It wasn't the recreational origami we think of today. That "play" origami didn't develop until the end of the nineteenth century. The ceremonial preciseness of paper folding reached Japan by the sixth century, and it was the Japanese who first called this new art form origami.

Overnight Mail

In 1970, the U.S. Post Office was the first to begin experimenting with overnight mail delivery. During this time, a new generation of wide-bodied or jumbo-jet transports began operations. The overnight possibilities wouldn't have been possible if not for the farsighted innovation and planning of the U.S. Post Office. Federal Express (FedEx) began shipping overnight packages in 1974, while Express Mail Next Day became a standard postal service in 1977. United Parcel Service (UPS) inaugurated its overnight delivery plan in 1985.

Pacemaker

On October 8, 1958, Dr. Ake Senning, a surgeon at the Karolinska Institute in Stockholm, Sweden, installed the first human implantable pacemaker. The patient was Arne Larsson, who lived until December 28, 2001, and had about two dozen pacemakers over his extended lifetime. That first pacemaker was developed by Dr. Rune Elmqvist. It had a pulse amplitude of 2 volts, a pulse width of 1.5 milliseconds, and supplied a constant rate of 70 to 80 impulses a minute. It was approximately 55 millimeters in diameter and 16 millimeters thick and was encapsulated in epoxy resin. The device's two NiCad battery cells were recharged weekly by beaming radio energy from an external device through the skin to the pacemaker's antenna.

Panda Born in Captivity

September 9, 1963, marked the birth date of modern times' first live birth of a giant panda born in captivity. The baby girl panda named Ming Ming was born at the Beijing Zoo, China, to parents Li Li (mother) and Pi Pi (father). China's attempts to breed pandas in captivity began in 1955, and in 1978, the Beijing Zoo was also the first to have a panda birth resulting from artificial insemination.

Paperback Book

On June 7, 1860, the first mass-marketed paperback book, *Malaseka: Indian Wife of the White Hunter,* was advertised in the *New York Tribune.* It was a work of fiction by Mrs. Ann S. Stephens and published by Irwin P. Beadle and Company of No. 141 William Street, New York City. Labeled as a "dime novel," the 128-page book sold for 10¢. The newspaper ad copy listed it as "Beadle's Dime Novels No. 1" to be ready Saturday morning, June 9, 1860.

Paperclip

Aside from the thirteenth-century European method of putting ribbon through parallel cuts in the upper-left corner of pages, the first paperclip is attributed to Johan Vaaler in 1899. Vaaler was a Norwegian inventor who was the first to patent a paperclip design. The patent said, "It consists of forming same of a spring material, such as a piece of wire, that is bent to a rectangular, triangular, or otherwise shaped hoop, the end parts of which wire piece form members or tongues lying side by side in contrary directions." This first paperclip was not curved like the common ones of today. That design didn't officially come into play until 1904, when Cushman and Denison, a New York City company, trademarked the Gem.

Paramedic

Around 100 B.C.E. in ancient Rome, aging Centurions were perhaps the first paramedics. The former military leaders had commanded a century of roughly 100 men and understood battlefield conditions. Aged and not able to fight, these first paramedics managed the injured soldiers, removing the wounded from the battlefield and performing some care. Although they weren't physicians, they had to stop bleedings, suture wounds, and complete amputations.

Passport

Aside from antiquity's letters, notes, and tax receipts that at times permitted safe passage, in 1414, King Henry V of England invented the first true passports, called Safe Conducts. The king wanted a means to help his subjects prove who they were in foreign lands. With the Safe Conducts, the King warned foreign people that they should allow his subjects to travel freely. No photographs were on these first passports, but they did contain a description of the holder. The official documents were foldable and were mainly issued for a very limited time and generally for a single journey.

Pencil

Modern pencils are the descendants of ancient writing instruments. Crude pencils can be traced back to the charred sticks of prehistoric times. With a blackened burnt stick, a caveman could make temporary markings on rocks or trees. Around 3500 B.C.E., the Sumerians used a stylus for inscribing marks on wet clay tablets. The stylus was made from sharpened reeds that honored their goddess of writing, Nissaba (originally their goddess of grass plants that included reeds). The ancient Egyptians used hollow pieces of reeds, bamboo, and tiny brushes of hair to mark on papyrus, a paperlike material made from plants. As early as 500 B.C.E., the Romans wrote with a thin metal rod that left a light but readable mark. Some of these early rods were made from a kind of lead. That made the Romans history's first people to use a "lead" pencil. It's not certain what culture may have called their writing tool a *pencillus*, Latin for "little tail," as the term arrived later (with no exact date or credit). But it's definite that *pencillus* is where our modern *pencil* comes from.

Penicillin

In 1896, 32 years before Alexander Fleming revealed the antibiotic properties of penicillin, French medical student Ernest Duchesne noticed that certain molds kill bacteria. Duchesne's research on the first penicillin went relatively unnoticed. In 1897, he submitted a thesis to get his doctorate degree from the Military Health Service School of Lyon. His thesis described the first "penicillin," but it wasn't called or named that at the time. The thesis was on the therapeutic capabilities of molds resulting from their antimicrobial activity.

Pension Plan

The first pension plan was passed in early 1776 prior to the signing of the Declaration of Independence. It was a national pension program for soldiers, although it really wasn't fully instigated until the time immediately following the Civil War. This pension plan went to one special segment of the American population—the disabled and/or survivors of deceased breadwinners. Following the Civil War, the program issued monthly checks to the North and the South's hundreds of thousands of widows, orphans, and disabled veterans. The creation of the Civil War pensions was the first time a full-fledged pension system was developed and executed. It also was America's first Social Security program.

Person Buried on the Moon

Although no one attended the ceremony, the first human burial on the moon took place on July 31, 1999, when a small container holding 1 ounce of the ashes of astro-geologist Eugene M. Shoemaker arrived near the south pole of the moon after a controlled crash. The ashes were aboard a NASA lunar prospector probe that had been launched in January 1998. This special first moon burial was arranged by Space Services, Inc., of Houston, Texas. Shoemaker died on July 18, 1997, and as the codiscoverer of Comet Shoemaker-Levy 9 in 1993, it seemed fitting to those he left behind to honor him by launching part of his remains into space for eternity.

Pesticide

Around 2500 B.C.E., the first-known pesticide was sulfur dusting. This first pesticide was used in Sumeria in ancient Mesopotamia. The Sumerians ignited the sulfur and used the fumes and dust from its combustion to spread over their crops as an insecticide and pesticide. The early civilizations were able to meet their meager needs from the easily mined native sulfur deposits near active and extinct volcanoes. Sulfur is also known as brimstone in its natural state and is a yellow nonmetallic element. The ancients also believed that burning sulfur cleansed the air of evil.

Pet Cemetery

In 1896, veterinarian Dr. Samuel Johnson founded the Hartsdale Canine Cemetery in Hartsdale, New York. A distressed client of Dr. Johnson had called his New York City office to say her dog had died and that she wanted to give it a proper burial. The problem—there was no way for this to be conducted legally in the city of New York. The compassionate doctor informed her that if she wanted to make the trip up to Hartsdale, located about 20 miles north of New York City, he'd be pleased to allow her to bury the animal in his apple orchard. That kind gesture served as the cornerstone of what was to become the world's first pet cemetery. Now called the Hartsdale Pet Cemetery and Crematory, it is the final resting place of more than 70,000 beloved pets.

Pet Food

Before the arrival of pet foods as we know them today, most dogs and cats lived off grains, meats, table scraps, and homemade food from their owners. It wasn't until 1860 that an electrician, James Spratt of

Cincinnati, Ohio, who was living in London at the time, created a biscuit made of wheat and vegetables mixed with beef blood. He had conceived the idea as he watched dogs around a shipyard eating scraps of discarded biscuits. His "Spratt's Patent Meat Fibrine Dog Cakes" were made and successfully sold in England some 30 years before they reached U.S. stores.

Pet Rock

As the story goes, Gary Dahl, a California advertising man, purchased what was to become the first pet rock, a Rosarita Beach stone (a rounded gray pebble) at a builder's supply store in San Jose, California, in April 1975 for 1 penny. Later, when Dahl was having drinks with his buddies one night, the conversation turned to pets. Dahl told them he had a pet rock and that it was an ideal pet—easy, cheap, and with a great personality. Afterward, Dahl spent 2 weeks writing the *Pet Rock Training Manual*, a step-by-step guide to having a happy relationship with the ecological pet. He next packed his pet rock in a gift box shaped like a pet carrying case and included the instruction book. About a month later, in June 1975, Dahl's pet rock hit store shelves. Retailing at $3.95, the pet rock fad spread like wildfire to the rest of the country and made Dahl an instant millionaire.

Petroleum Jelly

In 1859, the raw material for the first petroleum jelly was discovered in Titusville, Pennsylvania. The paraffin-like material was found sticking to some of the first oil rigs. Although it caused the rigs to seize, the workers used the rod wax, as they called it, on their cuts and burns because it hastened healing. Robert Chesebrough, a young chemist, discovered that by distilling the lighter, thinner oil products from the rod wax, he could create a light-colored gel. He opened his first petroleum jelly factory in 1870 in Brooklyn, New York. Chesebrough received a patent in 1872 and named his new product Vaseline.

Pharmacist

Around 700 C.E. in ancient Japan, men filled roles comparable to modern-day pharmacists. These first pharmacists mixed medicines, prepared compresses, and produced concoctions of herbs and plants. They performed their craft for the ill and injured, but especially for the high command of imperial royalty. Their place in the Japanese society was settled in the Taihō Code of 701 C.E., which was an administrative element of procedures in the Japanese code of ethics and government. These early pharmacists were highly respected and assigned a status superior to many others.

Photocopier

On October 22, 1938, Chester Floyd Carlson of New York City, a patent attorney and part-time inventor, made the first electro-photographic image with his photocopier apparatus. The first photocopy was made on wax paper pressed against an electrostatically charged, sulfur-coated zinc plate dusted with fine dark powder. The resulting image read "10.-22.-38 ASTORIA." Carlson patented the process, which he called xerography, on October 6, 1942.

Photograph

In 1822, the first successful photographic image, called a heliograph, was captured by Frenchman Joseph Nicéphore Niépce. The photograph was taken as the *View from the Window at le Gras* and looked like the sides of shaded stone buildings on both the left and right with the horizon in the distance. Niépce was able to create a permanent image by exposing coated pewter plates to a camera image and then using the vapors from heated iodine crystals to darken the silver. The exposure time for this first photograph lasted 8 hours. In the photo, the sun appears to shine on both sides of the building(s) because the sun had moved from east to west during the day.

Photojournalist

The first photojournalist was a Romanian-based photographer, Carol de Szathmari, who lived and worked during the Crimean War of 1853 to 1856. He took his camera to the war's battlefields along with a horse-drawn wagon specially equipped with a dark room for processing pictures. In April 1854, he and his wagon became a target for the Turkish artillery from Oltenitza, a Romanian city. They thought he was a Russian spy, and luckily they missed as he continued his work. His collections of photographs received a great deal of worldwide attention and many awards. In October 1857, one of his photo images appeared in the French magazine *Le Monde Illustre.*

Piano

Around 1720, Bartolomeo Cristofori of Padua, Italy, developed the first piano, known as a pianoforte. Cristofori came up with the idea to produce loud and soft notes and to maintain dynamic variety from the same instrument. He improved upon earlier attempts in other instruments with his idea to strike the pianoforte's strings with hammers that fell back from the strings after striking. This action was so fluid that one could play many repeated notes quickly and with a variety of tone. Cristofori produced about 20 of his pianos. They did not have legs but could be placed on a table or countertop for playing.

Pinball Game Machine

The "improved" Bagatelle-Table patented in 1871 is acknowledged as the ancestor of all pinball machines. British inventor Montague Redgrave manufactured the game at his factory in Cincinnati, Ohio. The original and older Bagatelle used a skinny, poollike table, ball, and cups at one end. Redgrave's improved version made the game much smaller so it could sit on a bar or countertop. He also added a coiled spring and plunger, replaced the large bagatelle balls with marbles, and added an inclined playfield. By pulling back and releasing the plunger, the player could shoot balls up the inclined playfield, a device that remains to this day. Redgrave's innovations in game design are acknowledged as the birth of modern pinball.

Planetarium

The first planetarium of note was the Globe of Gottorf, completed in 1664. It was constructed by Adam Olearius and Andreas Busch, who were residents of Frederick III, Duke of Holstein-Gottorf (now in Germany). The hollow celestial sphere measured about 10 feet in diameter and had a gilded star map on its interior. It weighed $3\frac{1}{2}$ tons and could seat several persons on a circular bench. Water-driven gears powered the device, which rotated once a day. This marvel of contemporary craftsmanship was placed in a palace garden to amuse and amaze visitors.

Playing Cards

During the Tang dynasty and no later than the ninth century, the Chinese began using tree leaves in simple card games. It's been documented that Princess Tongchang, daughter of Emperor Yizong of Tang, played leaf games with members of the Wei clan to pass the time. Years later, and with the simultaneous development of sheets of paper instead of paper rolls, paper dominoes were shuffled and dealt. Some experts suggest the first playing cards were actual paper currency, so in card games, you were playing both with and for the cards.

Poet Laureate

In 1616, the concept of a poet laureate originated in England. Benjamin Jonson, a playwright and lyrical poet from Westminster, London, became the first poet laureate, although unofficially. King James I created the position and granted Jonson an annual pension for his literary services to the crown. The office of poet laureate was a development from the practice when minstrels and versifiers formed part of the king's entourage, and Jonson was always on call to perform and create poetic greetings and readings.

Pogo Stick

George Hansburg, an Illinois baby furniture and toy designer, patented the first Pogo Stick in 1919. The early Pogos were wooden sticks with right-angled short planks for the feet that, Hansburg found, rotted and warped rather quickly. Hansburg improved the design and created a painted all-metal, enclosed-spring Pogo Stick with handles. He manu-factured them in an Elmhurst, New York factory, and as an advertising ploy, he taught the girls of the *Ziegfeld Follies* how to Pogo. The Roaring '20s proved to be the height of popularity for Pogo Sticks, and all kinds of stunts were performed using them—including a marriage ceremony!

Police Department

In ancient Rome, from around 27 B.C.E. through the next 200 to 300 years, the Praetorian Guard was the world's first organized police force or department. Instituted by Augustus Caesar as a protective organization for the use of military bodies as guardians of the peace, the Praetorian Guard protected the monarchs, although they at times corruptly assisted in the assassination of leaders. The guards' duties were often extended as they kept order of the mobs of Rome and the intrigues of the Senate in line. Although deceitful at times, this first police department helped give the Roman Empire much-needed stability.

Political Party

Around 621 B.C.E., in ancient Greece, the format within the Ecclesia was the birth of the world's first political parties. The Ecclesia was a citizens' assembly for the discussion of city policy and affairs. All citizens were permitted to attend, but the poorest could not address the assembly or run for office. The groups or pockets of ones within the Ecclesia who believed the same things and tried to push their beliefs and doctrines were the first political parties. They were loosely named from the leaders of the inner groups, such as *so-and-so*'s (leader's name) followers. Their political party may have supported a certain political figure, wanted to advance a particular policy, or make a general ideological stand.

Polka

In 1834, a peasant girl named Anna Slezak invented the polka dance for her own amusement in Labska Tynice, Bohemia (later Czechoslovakia). She called the dance steps *Madera* and created them to the tune of a folk song called "Strycek Nimra Koupil Simla" ("Uncle Nimra Brought a White Horse"). The dance soon became known as the polka from the Czech word *pulka*, which meant "half-step," and thanks to its liveliness and the rapid shift from one foot to another, the dance soon caught on.

Polyester

In 1941, the first man-made polyester was a fiber called Terylene. It began as a group of polymers in Wallace Carothers's DuPont chemical laboratory in Wilmington, Delaware. Carothers had discovered that alcohols and carboxyl acids could be successfully combined to form fibers. The work got put on the back burner after he discovered nylon (introduced in 1938). In 1939, a group of scientists at the Calico Printers Association in Great Britain took up Carothers's work. After a couple years of further research, they created the first polyester fiber.

Pop Music Chart

On January 4, 1936, *Billboard* magazine published its first pop music "Hit Parade," a list of popular tunes and instrumentals (not a list of records). The first number one song was "Stop! Look! Listen!" by Joe Venuti, a jazz violinist. The direct ancestor of the Top 40 concept, Hit Parade was created as a result of the development and expansion of radio plus the production of phonograph records and jukeboxes. The hit tunes were originally published in sheet music format and were typically recorded by several different artists. Each record company promoted its own version.

Popcorn

In the 1940s, Harvard archaeology students discovered the oldest-known ears of popcorn, dating to 4,000 to 5,000 years ago, in the Bat Cave of west-central New Mexico. The partially popped kernels ranged from smaller than a penny to about 2 inches in size. Popcorn later became prevalent in early sixteenth-century Aztec Indian ceremonies. In the 1850s, farmers in the American Midwest made common use of the moldboard plow, which led to the widespread planting of flint or popping corn. Called Prairie Gold, the crop became an important commodity around 1890. The first commercial producer was the Albert Dickinson Company of Odebolt, Iowa.

Popsicle

In 1905, 11-year-old Frank Epperson of San Francisco, California, accidentally left his fruit drink with a stirring stick in it outside on a cold night and it froze. The next morning, when he tugged on the stirring stick, out popped the world's first fruit-flavored icicle. Epperson christened his treat an Epsicle, and it quickly became popular with his school friends. Epperson waited 18 years before releasing his frozen treat to the public and changed the name to Popsicle after his children's frequent requests for "pop's sicle." Epperson received a patent for "frozen ice on a stick" in 1924.

Popular Election

Around 570 B.C.E., the first true popular elections were developed in the Greek city-state of Athens and the surrounding territory of Attica.

Under the leadership of Solon, the founder of democratic principles, a constitution was established that gave voting power to a popular assembly of freeborn male citizens. This popular assembly voted directly in elections for select public officials, on legislation, and on execution bills.

Post Office

Although the origins of a postal system date to antiquity, the General Post Office (GPO) was officially established in 1660 in England, by Charles II. Soon the GPO became a series of general post offices established across the British Empire. These first post offices were under the control of one Postmaster General and became the ancestor of the post office as it is known today. The first postmaster general of the GPO was Colonel Henry Bishop, who served from 1660 to 1663.

Postage Stamp

The penny black, the first postage stamp to be affixed to letters as a sign of prepayment, went on sale May 1, 1840, in London, England. The 1¢ stamps were printed in sheets of 240 on gummed paper. They weren't perforated, so they had to be separated by using scissors or a knife. A profile of Queen Victoria was printed on each of the 68,158,080 penny blacks issued. The stamps were the conception of Sir Rowland Hill, a postal reformer who convinced Britain to adopt the new system more reliable than the previous "honor system" delivery. Needless to say, it worked.

Potato Chip

In 1853, Native American George Crum was a chef at a Saratoga Springs, New York, resort when a customer complained that his french-fried potatoes were too thick. So out of spite, he fried up a serving of paper-thin potatoes cooked to a crunchy-crisp texture, which, to Crum's dismay perhaps, the patron immensely enjoyed. The so-called Saratoga

Chips became an instant hit with diners. To prepare, potatoes were tediously peeled and sliced by hand and soon packaged and sold, first locally, then throughout the New England area. The invention of the mechanical potato peeler in the 1920s paved the way for potato chips to soar from a small specialty item to a top-selling nationwide snack food. Potato chips are now the world's number one snack choice.

Presidential Inaugural Ball, Children's

On Sunday, January 18, 2009, in the run-up to the inauguration of President Barack Obama, a free gala was held for children who likely wouldn't attend the more grown-up balls on inauguration day. Held at the Historical Society of Washington, D.C., nearly 1,200 of the total 2,000 guests were children. Entertainment included the Nationals' and Capitals' mascots (from baseball and hockey), "Presidents" George and Abe, and penguins of Every Child Matters. Puppet shows, live music and magic, story times, face painting, balloon sculpting, mini classes, and exhibits were also available. Throughout the ball, carnival-inspired food like ice-cream novelties, popcorn, cotton candy, corn dogs, soft pretzels, cookies, and fruit was served.

Presidential Inaugural Ball, Neighborhood

On January 20, 2009, President Barack Obama held the first-ever Neighborhood Inaugural Ball. The open-to-the-public event was held at Washington, D.C.'s Convention Center. It was a star-studded event that included Beyoncé Knowles, Jay-Z, Ray Romano, Mary J. Blige, Maroon 5, Jamie Foxx, Nick Cannon, Mariah Carey, Keri Washington, and more. The new President and First Lady Obama danced their first dance serenaded by Beyoncé Knowles.

Presidential Hotline

On August 30, 1963, a direct telephone line between Moscow and Washington, D.C., was put into service. Its goal was to speed communication between the governments of the United States and the Soviet Union to help prevent the possibility of an accidental nuclear war, especially after the near catastrophe surrounding the October 1962 Cuban Missile Crisis. American teletype machines were installed in the Pentagon (not the White House), and the two countries exchanged encoding devices to decipher teletype (not voice) communications along the 10,000-mile-long cable. The first test message generated from the United States was "The quick brown fox jumped over the lazy dog's back 1234567890."

Presidential Pardon

In 1795, President George Washington issued the first presidential pardon, which was also the first pardon that overturned an impending death sentence. Washington pardoned and granted amnesty to hundreds of citizens who had been found guilty of participating in an armed rebellion to protest high alcohol taxes Congress had placed on whiskey sales. Putting down the Whiskey Rebellion of western Pennsylvania was one of the first tests of the new U.S. government.

Printing Press

German goldsmith and inventor Johannes Gutenberg began working on the first printing press in 1436, although it wasn't until 1439 that an official record exists. Gutenberg was living and working at the time in Strassburg (now Strasbourg, France). He modified earlier printing attempts, as well as utilized ideas from presses for making cheese, wine, and oil. His printing press used individual wooden (later metal) type fonts (movable type) that were laid flat and in word-making order on a wooden plate. The paper for the words to appear upon was pressed down with a heavy screw that was turned by a handle. On September 30, 1452, the Gutenberg Bible was published. It was the first book to be published in volume using movable type.

Prisoner-of-War Camp

In 1797, the first purposely built prisoner-of-war camp was established at Norman Cross, England, and housed prisoners captured in naval engagements from the French Revolutionary and the Napoleonic Wars. The camp was located on a 40-acre field purchased by the English government. Five hundred carpenters and laborers constructed buildings, storage sheds, officers' quarters, prisoner barracks, a series of inner surrounding walls, and an outside main wall and gatehouse. Around 30 wells were sunk to draw drinking water. This first prisoner-of-war camp could hold 5,000 to 6,000 prisoners.

Pro Basketball Team

The first professional basketball team was really two YMCA teams, one from Trenton, New Jersey, and the other from Brooklyn, New York, when they played each other on November 7, 1896. An admission fee was charged to spectators, and each player on both squads received $15 except for Trenton's star player, Fred Cooper, who got $16. There were 9 players on the floor at a time for each team. This first-known professional game was played at the Trenton Masonic Temple to a packed house. The Trenton YMCA squad defeated the Brooklyn YMCA team with a score of 15–1.

Pro Football Team

In 1896, the Allegheny (Pennsylvania) Athletic Association team fielded the first completely professional football team, which played an abbreviated two-game season. The team defeated squads from the Pittsburgh Athletic Club and the Duquesne Country and Athletic Club (also of

Pittsburgh) on consecutive days, winning both games by shutouts. The first pro football team's colors were blue and white and used Three A's as its nickname. Knowing that it would soon be barred from further competition by the Amateur Athletic Union, the Allegheny Athletic Association defiantly emptied its treasury to import a team of all-stars, including William "Pudge" Heffelfinger, the first openly professional player. After the two-game season, the sport was dropped from the club due to the "pro" football turmoil.

Pro Men's Baseball Team

In 1869, the Cincinnati Red Stockings became the first men's baseball team to publicly announce that their players were paid, making them the first professional team. Aaron B. Champion, a 26-year-old attorney, organized the team, mostly made of New Yorkers, with financing via a group of Ohio investors. The total payroll for the 1869 season was $9,300, with salaries ranging from $800 to a high of $1,400; the lone sub made $600. The Red Stockings also became the first team to travel across the United States with its players signed and bound to a club for the entire season. During their first season, the Red Stockings went 65–0.

Probation Officer

In 1841, shoemaker John Augustus was the world's first probation officer. The Boston, Massachusetts, resident volunteered to help drunks, vagrants, and petty thieves better themselves. His first case came about when he asked a judge to put a drunk in his care. When the drunk returned to the court after a period of probation under Augustus's heed, no one believed the drunk was the same man. He had undergone a complete turnaround for the better, thanks to Augustus's guidance. Although Augustus never got paid for years of service, he continued his work until his death in 1859.

In 1878, the Massachusetts's general assembly authorized the mayor of Boston to hire a probation officer based on the work of the late criminal justice reformer. Between the times of Augustus's death and an official hiring in 1878, numerous unofficial unpaid volunteers conducted probation affairs.

Prosthetic

The first prosthetic, a toe, dates to 1069 to 664 B.C.E. and is credited to the ancient Egyptians. The prosthetic toe, believed to have belonged to a 50- to 60-year-old woman, was found in a tomb near the city of Thebes, Egypt. Archaeologists speculate the prosthetic came about as the result of the woman losing her real toe due to complications from diabetes. The wood and leather prosthetic toe was held in place by leather strapping and jointed in three places so it could bend. It was apparently fully functional and aided walking and balance because it showed signs of wear. The amputation area behind the prosthetic was well healed.

Public Hospital

Around 400 B.C.E., the first public hospital was founded in Rome, Italy, by Fabiola, a Christian woman of noble birth who became the sole possessor of an affluent fortune on the death of her husband. With her fortune, she built an infirmary for the reception of the sick and homeless, where they were supplied with every comfort. She forsook her luxurious lifestyle and helped nurse the sick herself. The hospital was free for its patients, and some sources credit her as being the first woman surgeon.

Public Library

The first public library of sorts was an archive of more than 23,600 clay tablets covered with cuneiform writings (wedge-shape impressions) dating from around 2285 B.C.E. and discovered in 1933 at the site of the ancient Mesopotamian city of Mari (present-day Tall Hariri, Syria). The first U.S. public library was founded on November 16, 1700. The South Carolina General Assembly passed a law that established the St. Philip's

Church Parsonage Provincial Library in Charles Town and provided for its governance. The library remained in operation for 14 years.

Public Museum

Around 530 B.C.E. in Ur (part of modern-day Iraq), an educational museum containing a collection of labeled antiquities was founded by Ennigaldi-Nanna, the daughter of Nabonidus, the last king of Babylonia. Some of the museum's artifacts included a Kassite boundary marker, a piece of a statue of King Shulgi, and a clay cone that had been part of a building at Larsa. Along with them were clay cylinders that identified the objects in three languages. Ennigaldi-Nanna served as high priestess and ran a scribal school for upper-class women. The museum was the perfect complement for the school as a public display of esteem.

Public Park

Around 1175 B.C.E., the Egyptian pharaoh Ramses III commissioned numerous public gardens and parks. These first parks had wide places for walking that passed through plantings of flowers and fruit trees. Describing one of his parks, Ramses III said (according to records discovered in his mortuary temple at Medinet Habu), "I dug a lake before it … planted trees and vegetation … It was surrounded with gardens and arbor-areas filled with fruit and flowers." In addition to the public parks that he donated to the temples of his kingdom, Ramses III was benefactor to many of the public buildings of the era.

Public School

In 1543, Maurice, Duke of Saxony, established the first public schools of note in the southeastern part of present-day Germany. He donated the three major school facilities (Prince Schools, Meissen, and Grimma) in various cities to the New National Order that included public education after he had confiscated various properties during a warring conflict and sold them at enormous profits. With the monies and the inspirational help of Philipp Melanchthon, a German professor and friend of Lutheran church founder Martin Luther, Maurice's newly established schools provided literacy for the children of laborers and farmers. These first public schools enabled ordinary students to read the Bible.

Pull-Tab Can

The pull-tab or zip-top can was born in 1959 in Dayton, Ohio. Ermal Fraze, a tool-and-die maker, used the material in the lid of the can to form a rivet to hold a tab in place. His challenge was to notch an opening into the can's top the consumer could easily remove, but one still strong enough to withstand the can's internal pressure. Thanks to his clever engineering and workable concept, Fraze came up with a solution and later sold the rights to Alcoa. Alcoa convinced the Iron City Brewing Company in Pittsburgh, Pennsylvania, to give the new pull-tabs a test. In March 1962, the first pull-tabs were made available to the public on Iron City Beer. This first design had sharp edges on both the tab and the opening, and customers complained about cut fingers and lips. Improvements were made to fix the problems, and pull-tabs enjoyed decades of service until they were replaced on many soda cans in 1975.

Punch Clock

On November 20, 1888, Willard Bundy, a jeweler in Auburn, New York, invented the first punch clock. Also called a time clock, it was a mechanical timepiece used to track the hours an employee worked, which formed an official record to calculate an employee's pay. At the beginning and ending of work, the employee "punched the clock" by inserting an assigned heavy paper card into a slot, and time and day information were printed on the card. In 1889, Willard's brother, Harlow, organized the Bundy Manufacturing Company, which began successful mass production of the first punch clocks.

Purchase on Credit

In 1856, the first product available to be purchased on credit or on an installment plan was the sewing machine. The plan was made available from the Singer Sewing Machine Company of New York City. Edward Clark, the business partner of the company's founder, Isaac Singer, devised the innovative purchase plan. The arrangement allowed families who could not afford the lump sum $125 investment to purchase a sewing machine to pay monthly installments in the $3 to $5 range. At the time, the average yearly family income was about $500, and this first installment plan allowed households to get and use the product immediately. They were "buying on time," or paying for something while they were using it.

Purple Heart

General George Washington created the Purple Heart medal on August 7, 1782, to be awarded for "any singularly meritorious action." He called upon close friend M. Pierre Charles L'Enfant to design the award, which was originally called the Badge of Military Merit. Washington presented the "heart of purple cloth with a narrow lace or binding" to Sergeant Elijah Churchill on May 3, 1783. Churchill was cited for heroism in action regarding whaleboat raids in the several enterprises against Fort St. George in November 1780 and Fort Slongo in October 1781 on Long Island, New York. During a successful Fort Slongo raid against the British, Churchill was the only man wounded.

The Purple Heart as we know it today was reestablished in 1932 to coincide with the 200th anniversary of the birth of George Washington. Today's Purple Hearts are pins, medals, and/or variations of badges, depending on the military branch, but all have purple somewhere on them.

Quarantine

The first quarantine occurred around 1513 B.C.E. The Bible, in the Book of Leviticus, mentions the separation of the people infected with leprosy to prevent the further spread of the disease. The lepers were described as having blanched skin areas of some depth with whitened hair and were excluded from the community. Various verses from the Book of Leviticus further describe the quarantine: "The leper who has the disease shall wear torn clothes and let the hair of his head hang loose,

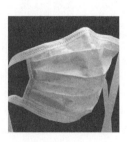

and he shall cover his upper lip and cry, 'Unclean, unclean.' He shall remain unclean as long as he has the disease; he is unclean; he shall dwell alone in a habitation outside the camp." (King James Version) Those who recovered were permitted to return to camp after completing rites of purification.

Quarry

During the Middle Paleolithic period in ancient Egypt about 40,000 years ago, stone from the Nile Valley was quarried by massive manpower and labor. The first quarries of this region consisted of pits and trenches for surface extraction of stones but also included vertical shafts and subterranean galleries. Limestone was the most commonly extracted stone, as it was utilized in huge quantities. Red, gray, and black granite were also mined. Hammerstones were used for the roughest stages, along with picks carved from the horns of gazelles and hartebeest for finer work. Without those mining operations and the backbreaking work of those first quarrymen, there would have been no great pyramids or grand temples constructed.

Quasar

In 1960, American astronomer Dr. Allan Rex Sandage made the first optical identification of a quasar, an extremely old and distant celestial object whose power output is several thousand times that of our entire galaxy. Assisted by his junior colleague, Thomas A. Matthews, at the Mount Wilson and Palomar Observatories in Palomar, California, Sandage recorded strong radio emissions generating from a localized direction in the sky that coincided with the position of a distant starlike object. This first identified quasar was located in the constellation Virgo. Describing the new object, Sandage probably coined the term *quasar* for "quasi-stellar radio source," although some say the term wasn't coined until 1964 in a *Physics Today* article by Chinese-born U.S. astrophysicist Hong-Yee Chiu.

Radar

On May 18, 1904, the first public demonstration of radar took place
at the Hohenzollern Bridge in Cologne, Germany. The radar had
been invented by a young engineer named Christian Huelsmeyer.
His telemobiloscope was a transmitter-receiver system for detecting
distant metallic objects by means of electrical waves. It worked well as
an anticollision device for ships. During the first demonstration, one
could hear a bell ringing as a ship approached on the river. The ringing
only stopped when the vessel changed direction or moved out of range
of the invisible beam generated from a wooden box placed onboard. The
device could detect ships up to 3,000 meters away. Although it worked
flawlessly, it aroused no major interest at the time.

Radio

Most consider Guglielmo Marconi the father of modern radio, but as
early as 1892, Nikola Tesla, a naturalized U.S. citizen from Yugoslavia
living in New York City, created the first basic radio design that worked.
Tesla discovered that he could transmit and receive powerful radio
signals via his newly developed coils when they were tuned to resonate
at the same frequency. Utilizing his Tesla coils in early 1895, he was
ready to transmit a signal 50 miles away, but a disastrous fire struck
and destroyed his lab. Only a few months after his death in 1943, the
Supreme Court of the United States credited Nikola Tesla as being the
inventor of the first radio.

Radio Station

In 1897, Guglielmo Marconi established the world's first radio station at the Needles battery on the western tip of the Isle of Wight, England. Marconi made most of his early experiments along the beautiful but deserted stretch of coastline because the area provided open water straight to the mainland, the optimum range of his equipment. Marconi's first radio station transmitted to two hired ferryboats and to another station in Bournemouth. The receivers did not take delivery of voice nor music, but instead received buzzing sounds created by a spark gap transmitter attempting to send a signal by Morse code.

Railroad

In Germany as early as 1550, the first railroads with raised rails, called wagon ways, were in use. (Earlier, around 600 B.C.E., the Greeks had wheeled vehicles that ran in grooves of limestone or in cut-stone tracks, although these weren't considered railroads.) The German wagon ways had tracks above or on top of the ground. These roads of rails were primitive and always in need of repair because the rails were constructed of wood. However, they did provide greater ease of movement than dirt roads and were used to transport tubs of ore to and from mines. Wagons or carts with special-made wheels were placed on the wooden rails and pulled by horses or pushed by men. These early wagon ways were the predecessors of the modern railroads.

Recycled Paper

In 1690, the first paper mill was established in the U.S. colonies, and with it, the first instance of paper recycling. The Rittenhouse Mill was founded near Germantown, Pennsylvania, by papermaker William Rittenhouse, printer William Bradford, and two wealthy Philadelphia businessmen. The mill made pressed paper from recycled waste paper and discarded rags. Thanks to an ever-increasing demand for books and writing material, older books were often bought, many times at auction, for the purpose of recycling the old paper into new paper.

Reflecting Telescope

In 1663, Scottish astronomer James Gregory came up with the design for a reflecting telescope, but it was Englishman Sir Isaac Newton who constructed the first practical reflecting telescope around 1668. Newton's design added a smaller diagonal mirror near the primary mirror's focus to reflect the image at a 90-degree angle. The user then could view the image without obstructing the incoming light. Newton donated the first reflecting telescope to the Royal Society of London around 1671.

Refrigerator

Although scores of inventors contributed many small advances in cooling machinery, it was 1834 when an American inventor obtained the first patent for a refrigerating machine. Jacob Perkins, who was living and working in Great Britain at the time, actually built a prototype system that worked. This first refrigerator, housed in a wooden cabinet and about the size of modern refrigerators, used ether in a vapor-compression cycle. Perkins proved that vapors or gases may be liquefied when subjected to high pressure, and that led to cooling. His refrigerating machine could make artificial ice, although it really never gathered much interest because there was already a well-established natural ice industry.

Repeating Rifle

Patented in 1860, the Henry rifle gave one man the single power of a dozen marksmen. It was the first successful repeating rifle and later evolved into the famous Winchester line. The .44 caliber rimfire, lever-action, breech-loading repeating Henry rifle was conceived by American Benjamin Tyler Henry and produced in a plant in New Haven, Connecticut. His rifle was the first of the practical (as in small enough to carry comfortably), truly rapid-fire small arms. The Henry also played an important role during the Civil War's western theater.

Republic

The first republic, *Res Publica* (public matter), was a Roman republic founded around 509 B.C.E. at the time Rome was governed as a republic during the epoch between the Roman Kingdom and the Roman Empire. This era began after the overthrow of the Roman king of the Tarquin monarchy. The Roman Senate was already in place but was now supplemented by two annually elected magistrates and military leaders, called consuls, of which Lucius Junius Brutus was the first, that performed executive duties. This new Roman republic centered on the principles of a separation of powers and checks and balances. San Marino, founded in 301 C.E., bills itself as the oldest surviving constitutional republic in the world.

Restaurant

In 1765, the first restaurant to be called by that name was the Champ d'Oiseau in Paris, France. Tavern keeper Monsieur Boulanger opened this first restaurant and kept it centered on food, not alcohol, coffee, or tea. The bill of fare included sheep's feet simmered in a white sauce, soup, and broth. Over the door Boulanger advertised these dishes as *restaurants* (restoratives) and claimed they restored one's health. Customers came to the restaurant primarily to eat, which was a novelty of the era, as most ate their meals at home or at an inn if on an overnight stay.

Revolver

The first known revolver was a 1597 revolving arquebus. It was produced by Hans Stopler of Nuremberg, Germany, whose design was an improvement on an ill-fated Venetian matchlock version that dated to the 1540s. An arquebus was a sort of premusket handgun that fired by applying a burning match to a trigger. It used a snaphaunce lock, an early flintlock mechanism for igniting a charge of gunpowder. Its main problem was the loss of gas due to ill-fitting parts; this routinely caused stray sparks from the chamber being fired to find their way to other chambers, often with disastrous results, such as blowing up in the shooter's hand or face. The chamber was manually turned or revolved in preparation for the next firing, provided the arquebus had held together, and the gun had to be reprimed before it could be shot again.

Revolving Restaurant

La Ronde, the world's first revolving restaurant, opened in 1961 atop an office building fronting the Ala Moana Shopping Center in Honolulu, Hawaii. It was designed by John Graham, a Seattle, Washington, architect. La Ronde, which has since closed, was structured to completely rotate once every hour at the speed of $\frac{1}{2}$ mile per hour. Food was prepared in the kitchen one floor down and brought up to an immobile central service area by a dumbwaiter. In 1962, Graham was commissioned to design the Space Needle for the Seattle World's Fair, and he included a revolving restaurant in it, too. The Eye of the Needle was the world's second revolving restaurant. In 1964, Graham obtained the first U.S. patent for a revolving restaurant.

Robot

Around 400 B.C.E., Greek mathematician Archytas of Tarentum built a mechanical wooden bird that was propulsion-powered by steam or some type of compressed air system. This first robot was called the Pigeon

and was the first artificial, self-contained flying device. One of its experimental flights traveled more than 650 feet, but after it fell to the ground, it could not take off again without adjustments. In 1917, Czech playwright Karel Capek coined the term *robot* in his play *Opilek* as an expression for automation.

Rocket

In 1232 c.e., the rocket made its debut. It was a fire arrow created by the Chinese and used by the Chin Tartars for fighting off a Mongol assault during the Sung dynasty. The rockets were bamboo tubes, capped at one end, left open at the other, and attached to a long stick. When filled with gunpowder and ignited, the gunpowder's rapid burning produced hot gas in the tube that escaped out the open end and produced thrust. The stick the rocket was attached to acted as a simple guidance system, and the simple, X-shape cross the rocket reclined in also helped aim it.

Rodeo

A mixture of cattle wrangling and bull fighting dates to the sixteenth-century conquistadors, but the first rodeo, where a cash prize was awarded ($40), took place on July 4, 1883, in Pecos, Texas, one block south of the Pecos Courthouse. Admission was free, and rodeo-goers could watch local cowboys ride broncos and rope steers. The rodeo came about that day because of bets from NA, Lazy Y, and W ranches that each had the fastest steer ropers. The blue ribbons given out were cut by pocketknife from the new dress of a 4-year-old girl in the crowd. The best roper was Morg Livingston of NA Ranch.

Roller Coaster

In the 1600s, the first roller coasters—or the ancestors of the mechanized versions that would come later—were created in Russia, in the area that would become St. Petersburg. People rode down steep ice slides on large sleds made from either wood or ice blocks. At first they used icy mountain paths, but soon the ice slides became ramped wooden constructions—some reaching 70 to 80 feet in height—with a sheet of ice several inches thick covering the surface. Steps or stairs were attached to the back of the slide. Riders would shoot down the ramp, zip up the other side, and gradually slide down to the middle. Some of these

Russian ice slides stretched for hundreds of feet and accommodated many large sleds at once. Sand was placed at the end of the ride to slow down the coasters. The activity became so popular that Catherine the Great took part in it.

Roller Skates

Various sources report that in the early 1700s in Holland an unknown Dutchman liked ice skating so much (he needed to, for transportation on Holland's numerous frozen canals in the winter), he wanted to be able to do it in the summer, too. To skate on dry land, he nailed wooden spools to strips of wood and attached the strips of wood to his shoes with overlapping straps. The anonymous Dutchman and others who soon followed him on their own dry-land skates were nicknamed "skeelers."

Safety Match

Gustaf Erik Pasch was a Swedish inventor and chemistry professor in Stockholm who invented the first safety match and was granted a patent in 1844. Commercial manufacturing was soon started but stopped soon after problems arose with the quality of the striking surface and the prohibitively expensive cost to produce the red phosphorus. More than a decade later, in 1855, Johan Edvard Lundstrom, also of Sweden, improved on Pasch's design by creating a match that could only be safely lit off a special striking surface. Lundstrom's efforts produced the world's first commercially successful safety match.

Safety Pin

On April 10, 1849, Walter Hunt of New York City received a patent for the first safety pin. He called his invention, which only took him 3 hours of wire twisting to create, a dress pin. Story has it that he wanted to pay off a $15 debt to a friend, so he decided to invent something new. Hunt's first safety pin came from a piece of brass wire about 8 inches long. On one end he placed a clasp that held the point of the wire in place when it was squeezed together. Hunt sold the rights to the first safety pin for $400, paid back the $15 borrowed from a friend, and had $385 to spare.

Sales Tax

The ancient Romans were the first to impose a sales tax. Around 6 C.E., Augustus Caesar introduced a sales tax to maintain the *aerarium militaire*, a military treasury he instituted. Calling the taxing program the *centesima rerum venalium*, Caesar's policy was a 1 percent general sales tax collected on all goods purchased at auction.

Sandwich

Rabbi Hillel, the Elder, who lived in Jerusalem during the first century B.C.E., created the first recorded sandwich. Hillel sandwiched a mixture of chopped nuts, apples, spices, and wine between two matzohs (brittle, flat pieces of unleavened bread) to eat with bitter herbs. The first written record of the word *sandwich* appeared in the journal of English author Edward Gibbons on November 24, 1762. Gibbons had recorded seeing British politician John Montagu, the fourth Earl of Sandwich, seated in The Cocoa Tree, a fashionable gentlemen's gaming club in London. The cooks of the club invented the sandwich to serve Montagu, who habitually spent a full 24 hours at cards not wanting to leave the gaming table to eat. These first sandwiches were beef between slices of toast. The name caught on when others began to order "the same as Sandwich."

Satellite

On October 4, 1957, the Soviet Union successfully launched *Sputnik I*. The world's first man-made satellite was 22.8 inches in diameter—about the size of a beach ball—and weighed 183.9 pounds. *Sputnik I* took about 98 minutes to orbit the earth in an elliptical path and ushered in the start of the space age and the U.S.–USSR space race. Its purpose was to map the earth's surface, but the *Sputnik* launch also led directly to the creation of NASA, the National Aeronautics and Space Administration, on October 1, 1958.

Search Engine

In 1990, the first search engine created was called Archie, a name shortened from its originally intended name, Archives. Alan Emtage, a student at McGill University in Montreal, Canada, conceived and launched the search engine. Archie logged on to FTP (file transfer protocol) servers on an ever-growing list and made an index of what files were on the servers. It only did this process and updated itself monthly because processor time and bandwidth were still a fairly valuable commodity in 1990. Archie has since become relatively obsolete compared with subsequent search engines, but Archie servers still do exist.

Secret Service Agent

On July 5, 1865, William P. Wood became the first U.S. Secret Service agent selected to head the Treasury Department's newly established Secret Service agency. Shortly before this, and while still superintendent at the Old Capitol Prison in Washington, D.C., Wood was temporarily assigned to the Solicitor of the Treasury and given the responsibility of detecting and capturing counterfeiters. In the chaotic hours following Lincoln's shooting on April 14, 1865, Wood was the first to identify the assassin as John Wilkes Booth. However, it wasn't until 1901 that the Secret Service received its official mandate to provide presidential protection. That was after President William McKinley was shot on September 6, 1901.

Seminary

In Mexico City, Mexico, around 1535, the first seminary was housed in the small chapel of Santiago de Tlatelolco and its surrounding buildings. The seminary was founded by Spanish Franciscan Juan de Zumarraga, Mexico's first Roman Catholic bishop. Its tutors were the Franciscans who taught the gifted sons of the Aztec nobility. Bernardino de Sahagún, the great chronicler of the history of New Spain, was one of its most notable teachers.

Serial Killer

After committing his first murder in 1426, Frenchman Gille de Laval, the seigneur de Rais, abducted, raped, and murdered some 140 children, mostly young boys. He was the world's first serial killer of record, in acts not associated with war or conquest. De Laval was a widely respected knight and noted soldier who had served under Joan of Arc at Orleans. After his military retirement, rumors spread of sadistic and murderous doings in his castle. Public uneasiness over his crimes all over France grew until he was handed over for trial on charges of heresy and sorcery to an ecclesiastical court. De Laval fully confessed to his hideous crimes and was publicly hanged on the gibbet at Nantes, France, on October 26, 1440.

Sewing Machine

In 1830, Barthelemy Thimonnier of Amplepuis, France, invented the first practical and functional sewing machine. There had been earlier patents and attempts by others, but they had all malfunctioned. In 1831, Thimonnier, a tailor, obtained the contract to produce uniforms for the French army. Afterward, he was almost killed when a mob of other French tailors burned down his garment factory. They feared unemployment because Thimonnier's new invention used only one thread and a hooked needle that made the same chain stitch used with hand embroidering. Thimonnier's sewing machine was built almost entirely of wood and used a barbed needle.

Shopping Mall

In 1916, the first planned automobile-centered shopping mall, Market Square of Lake Forest, Illinois, a suburb of Chicago, opened to the public. Architect Arthur Aldis had persuaded the area's wealthy residents and investors to form the Lake Forest Improvement Trust to build Market Square. It was an integrated shopping complex of 28 stores,

12 office units, 30 apartments, a gymnasium, a clubhouse, and pleasant landscaping. Many Lake Forest residents owned cars, so the automobile was the central factor in the overall planning—the center had convenient parking, for example. The National Register of Historic Places has listed Market Square as the first planned shopping district or mall in the United States. It's still open today.

Ski Lift

On February 14, 1908, Robert Winterhalder inaugurated the first lift specifically made for skiers. Winterhalder, who owned a small hotel in Schollach, north of Titisee-Neustadt in the Black Forest of Germany, spent years testing his lift before allowing the public to use it. He had created a mechanical system to let people climb the slopes by sitting on a sled or by sliding up while standing on skis. Users held onto a continuously moving cable, which was powered by a hydroelectric rig (a water mill that turned an electric generator). The lift was about 920 feet long and passed by 5 specially constructed wooden towers on its relatively gentle ascent to the top of the mountain. The cost of a ticket was 1 mark for 10 rides.

Skyjacking

The first recorded skyjacking of an airplane took place in Arequipa, Peru, on February 21, 1931. Pilot Byron Rickards had taken off from Lima, Peru, in his Panagra Ford tri-motor plane and flown to the southern city of Arequipa. As he landed, a group of rebel soldiers surrounded and detained him. Rickards was ordered to fly his plane to destinations the hijackers gave him. He adamantly refused, and the hijackers took him and his plane as their prisoners. Rickards kept on refusing to lift off until March 2, when he was told that their revolution had been successfully concluded and that he was free to return to Lima as long as he took one of the hijackers with him. Rickards did just that and escaped bodily harm.

Skyscraper

Although there's no official definition or height above which a building may be clearly classified as a skyscraper, most agree that the Home Insurance Building in Chicago, Illinois, was the world's first modern skyscraper. Built in 1885 mostly as an office building, it was very tall for

its time. Architect-engineer William Le Baron Jenney designed and built the skyscraper, which was originally 10 stories tall and 138 feet high. Another two stories were added in 1890. It was also the world's first building to be entirely supported by a steel frame. It was demolished in 1931 to make way for another building.

Sliced Bread

Mankind has been cutting or pulling apart bread by hand for thousands of years, but mechanically presliced packaged bread has only been available since 1928. It was that year that Otto Frederick Rohwedder introduced it for sale to the public on July 7 in Chillicothe, Missouri. He had invented the first machine to slice bread, which not only sliced it evenly but also wrapped it. Customers marveled at Rohwedder's Sliced Kleen Maid Bread's handiness for making sandwiches and toast. In 1930, Wonder Bread began selling presliced bread, and soon thereafter, many other bakeries followed suit. Not long after, toaster sales skyrocketed, thanks to the now-standardized size of sliced bread. Without Rohwedder, no one could exclaim: "It's the greatest thing since sliced bread!"

Slot Machine

In 1891, Brooklyn, New York, manufacturing company Sittman and Pitt produced the first mechanical slot machine. It had a coin slot, and instead of reels, it had 5 drums that held 50 cards each. After a player inserted a nickel into the slot and pulled the lever, the cards spun in the drums. When the spinning stopped, five cards randomly lined up to form a poker hand, which was either an immediate winner or loser. There was no direct payout mechanism, but prizes were wholly dependent on what was offered at the local establishment. A pair of queens might win a free beer, three of a kind might be rewarded with an expensive cigar, two pair might bring the winner two free liquor drinks, etc. Many times the house bettered its odds by removing a couple cards from the decks of one or more drums.

Smoke Detector

In the late 1930s, Swiss physicist Walter Jaeger inadvertently invented the first smoke detector while trying to invent a sensor for poison gas. Jaeger expected that as gas entered the device's sensor, it would bind to ionized air molecules and alter an electric current. The device failed, as small concentrations of gas did not affect the sensor's conductivity. Story has it that a frustrated Jaeger lit up a cigarette and was soon surprised to notice that a meter on the instrument had registered a drop in current. The smoke particles had done what the poison gas could not. His experiment paved the way for the future of smoke detectors.

Sneaker

Plimsolls were the first rubber-soled shoes manufactured in the late 1800s, but they were not called sneakers. That name goes to Keds, the first rubber-soled shoes to debut and be mass marketed as canvas-top sneakers in 1917. The United States Rubber Company, which had been consolidated from nine smaller companies, was the first to offer the sneakers. Henry Nelson McKinney, an advertising agent for N. W. Ayer and Son, coined the word *sneakers* because the rubber sole made the shoe stealthy or quiet in a time when most other shoes made noise when the wearer walked.

Snowmobile

The first snowmobile was a workhorse power sled and snowplow patented by Joseph, William H., and Moses C. Runnoe of Crested Butte, Colorado, on March 24, 1896. The object of the Runnoe gentlemen's invention was "to produce a sled with a motor which may be driven over the snow or ice with sufficient power to haul a load after it or upon it, which has easy means of steering, and is adapted to support a steam-engine or other motor which is used for driving the sled." This first snowmobile had an endless track of chain and eight steel crossbars, and from its patent's drawings, it appeared to be an engineless framework for a later engine to be added. Although the patent examiners approved the mockup and issued patent #557,085, historians doubt that an actual working model, complete with engine, was produced at the time of the patent. It wasn't until years later that other inventors furthered the concept of the Runnoes' very first snowmobile.

Soap Opera

Painted Dreams was the first soap opera, so named because of the sponsorship of soap companies and manufacturers. *Painted Dreams* broadcast on the radio and debuted October 20, 1930, on WGN Radio in Chicago, Illinois. The 15-minute daily show was based on the relationship between Irish American widow Mother Moynihan and her unmarried daughter. The popular show broadcast during the day, mainly to a listening audience of housewives, and ran into the early 1940s. Irna Phillips, who worked for the radio station as an actress and a voice-over artist, created the show and acted in it. She went on to successfully create other radio soap operas and famous TV ones as well.

These Are My Children, which debuted on NBC on January 31, 1949, was the first TV soap opera to air on a major network.

Soapbox Derby

On August 19, 1934, the first soapbox derby race was held in Dayton, Ohio. As the first racing event for children, it utilized hand-crafted gravity-powered cars that started on a ramp on top of a hill. Myron Scott, a photographer for the *Dayton Daily News*, came up with the idea after snapping pictures of boys racing wooden crates with baby buggy wheels. The winner of the first soapbox derby was 11-year-old Bob Turner of Muncie, Indiana, who won $500 for first place. In 1935, the event was moved to Akron, Ohio, because of its more-hilly terrain—and the fact the *Akron Beacon-Journal* offered to build a permanent track for the youth racing classic.

Social Security Check Issued

The first recurring-monthly Social Security check, numbered 00-000-001, was issued to 65-year-old Ida May Fuller on January 31, 1940, in the amount of $22.54. Fuller filed her retirement claim on November 4, 1939, having worked under Social Security for almost 3 years. For processing, the claims were grouped in batches of 1,000, and a certification list for each batch was sent to the U.S. Treasury. Fuller's claim was the first one on the first certification list.

Spam E-Mail

On May 3, 1978, the first spam e-mail was sent over ARPAnet, the Defense Department's network that was the precursor to today's Internet. A marketing executive for Digital Equipment Corporation by the name of Gary Thuerk was the world's first e-mail spammer. He wanted to publicize two open house events, one in Los Angeles on May 9, and one in San Mateo on May 11, where his company's latest computers would be unveiled. Several hundred invitations were successfully sent to the ARPAnet members on the West Coast. The reaction was mainly negative, but it did generate more attendees that turned into sales at the open houses.

Spandex

The first manufactured spandex fibers were produced as an experiment by Farbenfabriken Bayer, who earned a German patent for his synthesis in 1952. The final development of the fibers was worked out elsewhere independently. In 1959, after a decade of research, DuPont scientist Joseph C. Shivers invented a more advanced and sophisticated version than Bayer's early experiment. Although it was originally designated Fiber K, DuPont's marketing department came up with the trade name Lycra. That name distinguished DuPont's brand as the first manufactured spandex fiber. DuPont began full-scale manufacture of Lycra in 1962.

Speeding Ticket

On January 27, 1896, in Great Britain, the first automobile speeding ticket was issued to Walter Arnold, the pioneer of the petrol-engine car. He was driving through Paddock Wood in Kent at 8 miles per hour (mph)—four times the legal limit of 2 mph, which had been imposed for built-up areas. A policeman who cut short his lunch break, donned his helmet, and gave chase on his bicycle for some distance apprehended Arnold. Arnold was caught and fined 1 shilling. At the time there were only about 20 cars total in Great Britain.

Sperm Bank

In 1953, Jerome K. Sherman founded the world's first sperm bank in Iowa City, Iowa. A doctoral candidate student at the University of Iowa in the early 1950s, Sherman's extensive research led him to a method of successfully freezing and thawing sperm. With his work in cryobiology (the study of organisms and cells at sub-zero temperatures), Sherman took earlier scientific and related efforts to the next level. His methods made sperm banks possible, and it was from that first sperm bank that the first human birth resulting from the use of cryopreserved semen was realized.

Sport to Be Filmed

The first sport to be filmed was boxing, on June 14, 1894. Thomas Edison supervised the filming in his Black Maria studio on the grounds of his laboratory complex in West Orange, New Jersey. The boxing match was a sparring six-round contest between Mike "Beau Brummel" Leonard and Jack Cushing. The film featured hard fighting, clever hits, punches, leads, dodges, body blows, and slugging. Each round of the boxing contest was about 150 feet of film and lasted around 37 seconds. William Heise was the cameraman.

Sports Illustrated Sportsman of the Year

In 1954, the first *Sports Illustrated* Sportsman of the Year award went to track and field athlete Roger Bannister of Great Britain, the world's first person to run a sub 4-minute mile. Bannister received the award's trophy, a ceramic urn depicting Greek athletes, in January 1955. Since its inception in 1954, *Sports Illustrated* magazine has annually presented the award to "the athlete or team whose performance that year most embodies the spirit of sportsmanship and achievement." In 1972, tennis player Billie Jean King became the first female winner.

Sports Illustrated Swimsuit Edition

The first *Sports Illustrated* magazine swimsuit issue edition was dated January 20, 1964, and sold for 25¢. The cover featured model Babette March with a finger curled under her nose. She was wearing a white two-piece bathing suit and standing in nearly knee-deep water in the island surf of Cozumel, Mexico. The special issue was invented by *Sports Illustrated* editor Andre Laguerre along with fashion reporter Jule Campbell. This first swimsuit edition contained a five-page swimsuit model layout.

Sportswriter

The first sportswriter of considerable noteworthiness was Grantland Rice. After he graduated from Vanderbilt University in Nashville, Tennessee, in 1901, Rice worked various newspaper jobs. He saw sports as life itself and rose up as the subject's best-known and most respected writer. Recognized as a national sports authority, Rice's syndicated "Sportslight" column appeared in more than 100 newspapers. In 1924, Rice gave the backfield of Notre Dame's football team its legendary name, the "Four Horseman." He also coined the phrase "It was not important whether you won or lost, but how you played the game."

Stealth Aircraft

On October 21, 1947, the Northrop YB-49 became the first stealth aircraft. A prototype (at least nine others had been built), the "flying wing" could fly continually above 40,000 feet for as long as 6 hours. That height was beyond radar's normal and clearly verifiable airborne-targeting detection of the era. That made the Northrop YB-49 invisible, or stealth. The aircraft was designed and built by John Northrop, who modified the propeller-driven version of the post-WWII wing and equipped it with jet engines. The YB-49 had a range of 3,200 miles, a maximum speed of 495 miles per hour, and a wingspan of 172 feet. The plane's design had great promise, but several tragic accidents ensued, as the technology of the day was not capable of controlling the plane satisfactorily while in flight. The designers needed the computers that, unfortunately, wouldn't be available until some 20 years later.

Steam Engine

In 1698, Thomas Savery, an English military engineer and inventor, patented the first crude steam engine to solve the problem of pumping water out of coal mines. Savery described his machine as a "new invention for raising of water and occasioning motion to all sorts of mill work by the impellent force of fire." Savery's machine consisted of a steam boiler and a separate pumping vessel with an intake valve at the bottom. Steam under pressure forced the water upward and out of the mine shaft. Then a water sprinkler condensed the steam and created a vacuum, which sucked out more water. Savery's first steam engine could not work under extremely high pressure, thus lacking the power of later pumps.

Steamship

The first steamship to move under its own power was the *Pyroscaphe*, tested on the Saone River near Lyon, France, in 1783. Built by Claude-Francois-Dorothee, Marquis de Jouffroy d'Abbans, the *Pyroscaphe* was 138 feet long and fitted with a double ratchet mechanism that continuously rotated the paddle wheels. Its large and heavy steam engine moved the vessel upstream for about 15 minutes until the engine's vibrations broke the ship apart. After his patent application became indefinitely delayed, Jouffroy d'Abbans stopped his experiments. In 1807, American inventor Robert Fulton's *Clermont* steamship, although not the first to be built, was the first to become commercially successful. Fulton gave much credit to his predecessor Jouffroy d'Abbans.

Steel Bridge

Completed in 1874 with steel the primary structural material, the Eads Bridge in St. Louis became the first use of steel in a major bridge project. Still in operation, the bridge is a combined road and railway bridge over the Mississippi River that connects St. Louis, Missouri, and East St. Louis, Illinois. Named for its designer and builder, James B. Eads, the bridge's 500-foot ribbed steel arch spans were considered daring at the time. Due to its overall length of 6,442 feet, the Eads Bridge was also the first bridge to be built using cantilever (at only one end) support methods exclusively. During its construction, 15 workers died and 2 others were permanently disabled.

Steel-Frame Building

The first building entirely supported by a steel frame, and the first large-scale use of steel in a building, was the Home Insurance Building in Chicago, Illinois. Built by architect-engineer William Le Baron Jenney in 1885, the building was originally 10 stories tall and 138 feet high. Another two stories were added in 1890. The building's metal frame was completely encased in brick or clay-tile cladding for fire protection. Demolished in 1931 to make room for another building, it was also considered the world's first skyscraper.

Stock

Aside from antiquity's clay tokens used for accounting and financial purposes, the first company to issue stock was the Dutch East India Company (Dutch Vereinigte Oostindische Compaignie, or VOC) in 1602. A stock is a share of ownership in a company that can be bought, sold, or traded. The States-General of the Netherlands granted the trading company a 21-year monopoly to carry out colonial activities in Asia. By issuing and selling stock certificates, the Dutch East India Company remained an important trading concern that paid an 18 percent annual dividend to its stockholders for almost 200 years.

Stock Exchange

Around 1450, the Beurs Stock Exchange was founded in Bruges, Belgium. The exchange was established by the Van de Buerse family of financiers, brokers who kept an inn where financial transactions were concluded. Bankers gathered in front of their inn house to engage in securities trading. In the early sixteenth century, this flourishing period came to an end as the economic and commercial center moved to Antwerp, Belgium. The French word *bourse* is for "stock market," which derived from the Van de Buerse family name.

Stock Ticker

On November 15, 1867, the first stock ticker debuted in New York City, when Edward Calahan configured a telegraph machine to print stock quotes on streams of paper tape. The ticker device got its name from the sound its type wheel made. It ultimately revolutionized the stock market by making up-to-the-minute prices available to investors around the country. Calahan worked for the Gold and Stock Telegraph Company in New York. The company rented its tickers to brokerage houses and regional exchanges for a fee and then transmitted via telegraph the latest gold and stock prices to all its machines at the same time.

Submarine

In a series of trials between 1620 and 1624, Dutch inventor Cornelius J. Drebbel (Van Drebbel) built and demonstrated the world's first submarine. The craft's hull was a wooden frame skinned with greased leather and was powered by oars that protruded through flexible leather seals. It had a submergence time of several hours, thanks to snorkel air tubes running into the vessel and held above the surface by floats, and successfully maneuvered at depths of 12 to 16 feet during repeated trials in England's Thames River. Van Drebbel followed his first submarine with two other larger ones, but although his work was shown to King James I, it failed to arouse the British navy's interest.

Subway

The Metropolitan, the world's first subway, opened on January 10, 1863, in London, England. First proposed by City Solicitor Charles Pearson in 1843, builders completed the 3.75-mile underground railway between Farrington Street and Bishop's Road, Paddington, in less than 3 years. The subway was powered by steam locomotives that spewed tremendous amounts of sulfurous smoke into its tunnel, but the "underground" was an immediate success, attracting 30,000 riders on its first day of operation and 9,500,000 passengers in its first year.

Sulfa Drug

The first sulfonamide (sulfa drug) was trade named Prontosil. It began in 1932 as several experiments in the laboratories of the German company Bayer AG and was discovered and synthesized by a team under the general direction of Heinrich Hoerlein, Josef Klarer, and Gerhard Domagk. The team discovered that an azo dye, Prontosil, cured streptococcal infections in mice. The first official communication about the breakthrough discovery was not published until 1935. The dye-based Prontosil was the first medicine that could effectively treat a range of bacterial infections inside the body.

Sunscreen Product

Since ancient times in both Egypt and India, inorganic clays and mineral powders were used to protect the skin from the sun. But in 1938, Gletscher Crème became the first effective sunscreen. It was developed by a young Austrian chemistry student named Franz Greiter. While climbing Piz Buin, a mountain on the Swiss-Austrian border, Greiter had suffered severe sunburn. Afterward and with inspiration, he formulated a product that would protect the skin against the adverse effects of the sun. Greiter developed his crème, which would later become known as Piz Buin, in a small laboratory in his parents' home.

Super Glue

In 1942, Dr. Harry Coover discovered a substance called cyanoacrylate, the chemical name for what would later become super glue, while working for Kodak Research Laboratories in Rochester, New York. Coover was searching for materials to make clear plastic gun sights for WWII firearms and stumbled upon a substance that stuck to everything it came into contact with. Coover rejected his first super glue because it was *too* sticky. Later, in 1951, while supervising research at the Eastman Company in Kingsport, Tennessee, Coover finally realized that cyanoacrylate was, indeed, a useful product, but it wasn't until 1958 that the Eastman compound #910 was marketed and later packaged as super glue.

Superconductor

In 1911, the first superconductor known to physicists was mercury, discovered by Heike Kamerlingh Onnes, director of the Cryogenic Laboratory at the University of Leiden in the Netherlands. Superconductivity is a phenomenon occurring in certain materials at very low temperatures, characterized by no electrical resistance. Onnes studied the resistance of solid mercury at cryogenic temperatures using liquid helium as a refrigerant. He found that mercury cooled to 4.2 degrees Kelvin (about –269 degrees Celsius) exhibited almost no electrical resistance. In subsequent decades, superconductivity was found in several other materials, but mercury was the first.

Surfer

Around 2000 B.C.E., the Polynesians started surfing. This was around the time of their movement from Asia to the eastern Pacific.

The first-known surfer of the modern era was Duke Kahanamoku, who was born in Waikiki, Hawaii, in 1890. Along with his teenage friends, Kahanamoku formed the first-ever surf club known as Hui Nalu, but commonly called the Beach Boys of Waikiki. "The Duke," as he was called, became an Olympic champion swimmer and remains a symbol of Hawaii. He is known as "the father of surfing."

Synagogue

Around 597 B.C.E., according to tradition, the possible first synagogue was Shef ve-Yativ in Nehardea, a city of Babylonia. The first synagogues were very simple buildings and consisted of only one room with benches along the sides of the walls. But unlike temples, there were many of these smaller buildings in different locations. The oldest synagogues, and perhaps the first, probably arose where the Jews were slaves in Babylon (now modern Iraq), but specific details are not clearly known.

System of Measurement

The first system of measurement involved the human body of early man, a natural method for the ancients. During biblical times, the cubit was the length of a forearm or the distance from the tip of the elbow to the end of the middle finger. Half a cubit was called a span and was the distance across the hand from the tip of the thumb to the tip of the little finger. What is now called an inch was the width of a man's thumb. The distance across a man's outstretched arms equaled a fathom. The foot-rule started out as the length of a man's foot.

System of Writing

Around 3400 B.C.E., the first system of writing was picture writing. The ideographic style, which employed pictures as signifiers, was developed in Sumer (present-day southern Iraq) and was primarily used for accounting. This Sumerian picture writing called cuneiform included as many as 1,200 separate ideograms that represented a thing or concept rather than the word for it. The picture presentations were pressed into wet clay with the end of a reed, and the clay was dried to form tablets. The ancient Sumerians also wrote and devised arithmetic based on units of 10, the number of fingers on both hands.

Tank

Aside from Leonardo da Vinci's drawing of a round, tanklike armored wagon in the 1400s, Austrian Gunther Burstyn designed the first cross-country military tank in 1911. Burstyn was an engineering officer of the Austro-Hungarian Army and called his tank the *Motorgeschütz*, which literally meant "motor gun." It had a swiveling turret and was based on American agricultural tractors. Although it was a practical design, it was rejected by both the Austro-Hungarian and German empires.

Tap Dancer

During the 1840s, tap dancing became popular on the American minstrel circuit. William Henry Lane of Providence, Rhode Island, was the first tap dancer of renowned fame. He was an entertainer who went by the stage name Juba and was billed as the king of all dancers. Lane had mastered his steps by combining jigs and reels with West African giouba, a kind of lively rhythmic dance. He was also the first African American to be the headliner or top billing of a troupe of Caucasian American dancers.

Taxi Cab

In Germany in the early summer of 1897, the Daimler Victoria became the world's first dedicated taxi cab, equipped with the newly invented taximeter for calculating fare charges to customers. On June 26, 1896, the taxi had been special ordered by a Stuttgart-based haulage operator by the name of Friedrich Greiner from Daimler-Motoren-Gesellschaft in Cannstatt. Upon successful construction, the taxi was supplied to Greiner in May 1897 at the hefty price of 5,530 marks (around $50,000 today)—plus he had to pay rental for the taximeter. A heating system for the rear-seat passengers (another first) was installed in this first taxi, and it had a half-top feature that could be opened in fine weather. Greiner soon renamed his haulage outfit the Daimler Motorized Cab Company, becoming the world's first motorized taxi business. By 1899, the company had taken delivery of seven Daimler taxis.

Telegraph

On March 3, 1791, French brothers Claude and Ignace Chappe demonstrated the first telegraph. The nonelectrical air telegraph depended on line of sight for communication. The brothers constructed a chain of hilltop and manmade towers about 3 to 6 miles apart, each within the line of sight of two others via a telescope. The towers were outfitted with two wings or movable arms mounted on a crossbeam. By positioning the wings and tilting the crossbeam in different ways, they were able to transmit a coded message along the route of the towers. Different positions represented letters of the alphabet, common words, and numerals. Skilled signalers could transmit messages in a fraction of the time compared to messages delivered by horseback.

Telephone

Between 1850 and 1862, Italian American inventor Antonio Meucci developed at least 30 different models of the first working telephone. Although there's controversy from the Alexander Graham Bell camp, on June 15, 2002, the United States Congress officially recognized Meucci as the true inventor of the telephone. During the creation of the first telephones, Meucci was too poor to pay the fees to patent his inventions.

He had to settle for a legal notice called a caveat that stated he had invented the telephone. Meucci's first phones were crude and simple devices but could change sound to electricity and back again to sound.

Television

On September 7, 1927, the American inventor Philo T. Farnsworth demonstrated the world's first working television system with electronic scanning of both the pickup and display devices. Farnsworth, along with his wife and her brother, televised a straight line from one room to another in his San Francisco, California, lab to create the first fully electronic picture. Later that year, they transmitted a puff of cigarette smoke. Many inventors had written about, worked on, or built various electro-mechanical television systems prior to Farnsworth's demonstration, and the invention of the first television has been disputed adamantly throughout its history.

Tent Revival Meeting

Moses was the first person in history to deliver God's word using a tent as the focus of the community. He did so around 1500 B.C.E. in a portable tent called the Tabernacle. During a tent revival meeting, as told in the Book of Exodus, people gathered to worship and invite the presence of the Lord. The Tabernacle tent was pitched almost anywhere in the open air, and word of the revival meeting was spread by word of mouth. It wasn't until the 1700s that great itinerant preachers combed the countrysides in Europe and America with their tent revivals.

Toll Bridge

On May 3, 1654, the world's first toll bridge opened over the Newbury River in Rowley, Massachusetts. A minimal toll was probably collected primarily by the honor system, with a wooden toll box on both sides of the bridge. The toll was only for animals; pedestrians and riders were permitted free passage. The bridge was on the property of Richard Thorlo (or Thorla, Thorley, or Thurley, depending on the source). Born in England, Thorlo had relocated to the Massachusetts colony. The bridge, built with Thorlo's own money and toils to provide convenient passage, remained a toll bridge until 1680. The toll money was Thorlo's to keep.

Toothpaste in a Tube

In 1892, Dr. Sheffield's Creme Dentifrice was the first packaged toothpaste in a collapsible metal tube, or the compressible tube, as it was sometimes called. Dr. Washington Wentworth Sheffield, a New London, Connecticut, dentist, devised the successful idea. Previously, toothpaste was packaged in porcelain jars. To use, you simply dropped a toothbrush into the jar's paste and took what you needed ... but so did other family members. Sheffield's tube was both convenient and sanitary. Its air-tightness kept the toothpaste from drying out, while the collapsible tube packaging lowered the overall price of toothpaste and spawned the tooth-cleaning industry.

Top Hat

In 1797, London haberdasher John Hetherington invented the first top hat. The hat was a silk-covered exaggerated variation of a beaver-fur riding hat. It was tall, round, and cylindrical but flat on the top. Story has it that while wearing it, Hetherington was arrested for disturbing the peace by "appearing on the public highway wearing a tall structure of shining lustre and calculated to disturb timid people," according to newspaper reports. He was found guilty and fined a £500 bond.

Traffic Light

On December 10, 1868, the first traffic light was installed in London, England, at the intersection of George and Bridge Streets outside the British Houses of Parliament. It was a revolving gas-powered lantern with red and green signals. Invented by railroad signal engineer J. P. Knight to control the flow of horse buggies and pedestrians, it was fitted with a lever at the base that was manually turned so the appropriate light faced traffic—red for stop and green for go.

Transatlantic Nonstop Flight

On June 14 and 15, 1919, two British aviators, Captain John W. Alcock (pilot) and Lieutenant Arthur W. Brown (navigator), made the first non-stop flight across the Atlantic Ocean. They flew together in a converted twin-engine Vickers Vimy bomber 44 feet long and with a wingspan of 68 feet. The 1,890-mile flight was made in 16 hours, 27 minutes from Newfoundland, Canada, to Clifden, Galway, Ireland. During the trip, the men ate meat sandwiches and chocolate and drank coffee. They both brought along toy cats as mascots.

Transistor Radio

On October 18, 1954, the first transistor radio, the Regency TR-1, was announced, and it hit the consumer market the following month. At 11 ounces and 3×5×1¼ inches in its plastic case, the Regency TR-1 was developed by the Regency Division of I.D.E.A. (Industrial Development Engineering Associates) of Indianapolis, Indiana, and patented by Dr. Heinz De Koster, a Dutch Ph.D. employee of the company. It retailed for $49.95; came in various colors, including black, ivory, mandarin red, cloud gray, mahogany, and olive green; and sold about 150,000 units. The Regency TR-1 featured 4 germanium transistors that operated on a 22.5-volt battery that lasted about 20 hours.

Traveler's Check

In early January 1772, the London (England) Exchange Banking Company issued the first traveler's checks for use in 90 European cities. These first traveler's checks, conceived by Robert Harries, a banking official employed at the London Exchange Banking Company, replaced letters of credit, which were difficult to obtain. The circular notes with a value of $20 allowed travelers to exchange the traveler's check for local currency. They were guaranteed replaceable if lost or stolen.

Triathlon

On Wednesday, September 25, 1974, the first triathlon was held at Mission Bay in San Diego, California, directed and conceived by Jack Johnstone and Don Shanahan. The San Diego Track Club sponsored the event consisting of 6 miles of running (the longest continuous stretch was 2.8 miles), 5 miles of bicycle riding (all at once), and 500 yards of swimming (the longest continuous stretch was 250 yards). Approximately 2 miles of the running was barefoot on grass and sand. Participants brought their own bicycles, and each of the 46 contenders paid a $1 entry fee. Bill Phillips finished first with a time of 55 minutes, 44 seconds. All 46 entrants finished the event.

Tunnel

The world's first tunnel, the Middle Bronze Age Channel, dates to around 1800 B.C.E. and is located in Jerusalem, Israel. The tunnel was really a covered aqueduct in the ground that led from the Gihon Spring to the Pool of Siloam of ancient Jerusalem. This channel diverted the spring's water supply from outside the city's walls to the inside. It was a 20-foot-deep ditch that was covered over by large rock slabs after construction. The narrow tunnel was hidden by foliage that grew over and on it. Visitors can still walk most of its length.

Tuxedo

October 10, 1886, marked the first official appearance of the dinner jacket. It was at the Tuxedo Club's Autumn Ball in Tuxedo Park, New York. Pierre Lorillard IV, heir to a tobacco fortune and the largest landowner in town, introduced the first tuxedos from a variation of tailless red wool coats worn by English fox hunters. He had his tailor create four new formal tailless black jackets. Lorillard declined to wear the result, but his son Griswold and three of his friends wore them to the ball. The new style became known as "what they're wearing to dinner in Tuxedo," which earned those first four jackets the name "tuxedos."

TV Critic

Gilbert Seldes became the first TV critic of note with a 1937 article, "Errors of Television," published in the *Atlantic Monthly.* The distinguished writer and Harvard graduate was born in Alliance, New Jersey, and became well known for his 1924 book *The Seven Lively Arts,* a systematic critique of popular American culture. Seldes was the first to insist that popular culture, including TV, deserved serious attention from cultural critics.

TV Dinner

In 1949, Albert and Meyer Bernstein of Pittsburgh, Pennsylvania, marketed a line of frozen meals on three-part divided aluminum trays, but it was C.A. Swanson & Sons of Omaha, Nebraska, who first marketed and called its frozen meals TV dinners. The dinners cost 98¢ and consisted of turkey and cornbread dressing with gravy, sweet potatoes, and peas. Thanks to the aluminum tray the dinner came packaged in, you could just open the box and heat up the dinner in an oven. The convenience and ease of preparation made people who were not good cooks able to enjoy nearly any type of dinner they desired. The TV dinner was so

popular in its first year that it sold more than 10 million units. Swanson transformed its meals into a cultural icon via a massive advertising campaign. The company stopped calling them TV dinners in 1962, and in 1986, Campbell Soup (owner of Swanson) replaced the aluminum trays with plastic microwavable ones.

TV Evangelist

The first evangelist to appear on television was Fulton J. Sheen, a Roman Catholic archbishop born in El Paso, Illinois. Sheen successfully made the switch to TV in 1951 after a couple decades of popular radio broadcasts. His *Life Is Worth Living* program aired on the DuMont Television Network and later on ABC. The program consisted of Sheen simply speaking in front of a live audience. He often spoke on the theology of current topics, including the evils of communism, while occasionally using a chalkboard to stress key points. Sheen won an Emmy Award for Most Outstanding Television Personality in 1952.

TV Guide, National

Although *TV Guide* distributed regional issues as early as 1948, the first national version was released April 3, 1953, at a price of 15¢. The cover of volume 1, number 1 featured an unsmiling baby boy dressed in yellow. A headshot of Lucille Ball also appeared in the top-right corner over the headline "Lucy's $50,000,000 Baby." The baby, Desiderio Alberto Arnaz IV, was the first child of Lucille Ball and Desi Arnaz, born on January 19, 1953.

TV Interracial Kiss

On November 22, 1968, television's first interracial kiss aired on a *Star Trek* episode titled "Plato's Stepchildren" shown on NBC-TV. The kiss between characters Lieutenant Uhura and Captain Kirk, as played by African American Nichelle Nichols and Caucasian William Shatner, really wasn't a romantic moment, as space aliens were using mind control to force the characters to kiss against their will. Still, some U.S. TV stations refused to air the episode.

TV Mega-Hit Show

With its debut on June 8, 1948, *The Texaco Star Theater*, also known as *The Milton Berle Show*, was TV's first mega-hit show. Sponsored by the Texaco Oil Company, the show was enormously popular, and by November 1948, it had earned its highest rating of 86.7 percent of all TV households. This hour-long, comedy-variety NBC-TV series literally increased the sales of TV sets across the United States. Viewers *had* to see the show. Its comedic host, Milton Berle—or "Uncle Miltie," as he was called—earned the title of "Mr. Television" because of the way his show caught the public's imagination and influenced the growth of the medium. The show wound down in June 1956.

TV Remote Control

In 1950, Lazy Bones became the world's first television remote control. Created by the Zenith Radio Corporation of Lincolnshire, Illinois, the device could turn a television on and off and change channels by activating a motorized mechanical tuner on the TV it was linked to. Lazy Bones wasn't wireless, but rather attached to the television by a bulky cable. Consumers put up with the cable stretched out across the floor because they loved the convenience.

TV Series

On October 8, 1936, on the British Broadcasting Corporation (BBC) Television Service in Great Britain, *Picture Page* became the first TV series to be broadcast. It was also the first series to become a long-running and regular popular hit. The program was in a magazine format with 2-hour-long segments broadcast live each week. It featured interviews with famous personalities and offered a wide range of topics, including public events taking place. The main star was Canadian actress Joan Miller, who played the role of a switchboard operator. *Picture Page* ran from 1936 to 1939, took a hiatus during World War II, restarted in 1946, and ran until 1952.

TV Sitcom

Mary Kay and Johnny debuted as the first situation comedy, or sitcom, broadcast live on network TV on November 18, 1947, on the DuMont Television Network. The 15-minute-long weekly sitcom starred the real-life married couple of Mary Kay and Johnny Stearns, who also created and wrote all the scripts for the show. The program depicted the New York City apartment life of the title characters, a young married couple. During its almost 300 episodes, the show expanded to 30 minutes. CBS and later NBC also broadcast the show. The final episode aired March 11, 1950.

TV Talk Show

In 1942, *The Franklin Lacey Show* was TV's first talk show (even though some historians argue the first credit belongs to *The Tonight Show*, which premiered in 1952). Franklin Lacey was a lanky young writer who had his own talk show on California station W6XYZ. Although there were only 40 TV sets being watched at that time in the Los Angeles area, Lacey's talent glimmered as he interviewed local guests and talked about current events with some zaniness thrown in. Not much documentation remains about the show, but it was probably 30 minutes long and broadcast live daily for at least a couple years. Lacey went on to become an accomplished playwright.

U

Umbrella

The first umbrella goes back thousands of years to no exact dates. Early umbrellas were wide-leafed plants held over the head. Ancient drawings

depict the Egyptians using a device similar to an umbrella. The first umbrellas were not used to deflect rain, but were often carried by slaves to shade their masters from the sun. Around 2,000 years ago, the ancient Chinese waterproofed their parasols and created the first rain umbrella.

Umpire

On June 19, 1846, Alexander Jay Cartwright officiated a baseball contest between the Knickerbockers and the New York Nine at Elysian Field in Hoboken, New Jersey. The game was governed by his own "Cartwright's Rules," which were the first set of formal rules for baseball. The rules also laid out the sport's diamond-shape field and established the players' nine positions. During that first umpired game, Cartwright fined one player 6¢ for cursing. As the only umpire for the contest, Cartwright stood behind the pitcher to call balls and strikes and to make base calls. The New York Nine won the game 23–1 in 4 innings.

On June 3, 1953, the U.S. Congress officially credited Cartwright as the inventor of the modern game of baseball, debunking the popular myth Abner Doubleday had invented the game.

Vasectomy

In 1823, the first vasectomy was performed on a dog in the United Kingdom. It was 1830 when Sir Astley Cooper published the first study on the topic, "Observations on the Structure and Diseases of the Testis," at that same time. After the vasectomy was performed, it was observed later that the dog was able to have sex, yet unable to get other dogs pregnant. Cooper and his research assistants found out that despite shutting off the exit of the sperm, the testicles still produced sperm. The dog was killed for study 6 years later (in 1829), but its sperm was still being produced.

On October 12, 1899, Dr. Harry C. Sharp, as medical officer of the Jefferson Reformatory in Indiana, performed the first notable human vasectomy. The voluntary procedure, performed on a 19-year-old inmate by the last name of Clawson, was successful.

Vaudeville Show

With roots in British music halls and French comic operas, vaudeville's first clean variety show (early shows were a bit lewd and not family-friendly) was established in New York City by Tony Pastor in 1875. The show took place at the Metropolitan Theatre at 585 Broadway. In 1881, Pastor leased the Germania Theatre and renamed it Tony Pastor's New Fourteenth Street Theatre. This was where he achieved his greatest vaudeville success. Pastor is considered "the father of modern vaudeville" because he brought in unrelated acts featuring magicians, acrobats, comedians, trained animals, singers, and dancers. Pastor was a highly moral producer and actor who solicited family trade. He influenced other theater managers to follow suit.

VCR

In March 1956, the Ampex VRX-1000 was introduced at a price of $50,000. Although it was 9 feet long and weighed 900 pounds, it made tape recordings of TV signals practical for the first time. Developed by Ampex of Redwood, California, the device was a VTR, or video tape recorder. Unlike a VCR, or video cassette recorder, the VTR did not use a cassette, only the tape itself. In the fall of 1975, the first VCR for home use was the SONY Betamax SL-6200 (SL-6300 in Japan). The VCR was contained within the LV-1901 console of a 19-inch Sony Trinitron tele-

vision set. This package deal retailed for $2,495. In the spring of 1976, the Sony Betamax SL-7200 (SL-7300 in Japan) became the first fully domestic stand-alone VCR, complete with a built-in tuner, that could receive TV signals directly. It sold for $1,400. The biggest drawback to Betamax was that it could only record for 1 hour.

Velcro

The first Velcro was invented in 1948 by electrical engineer Georges de Mestral of Commugny, Switzerland. Velcro is the trademark name for a nylon fastener consisting of two strips of fabric that form a bond when pressed together. De Mestral had become curious about how prickly seed husks clung to his clothes and his dog's fur during hunting expeditions. He duplicated that bur principle to create a hook-and-loop fastener for garments. He received a patent for his invention in 1955.

Video Game

On October 18, 1958, William Higinbotham introduced his *Tennis for Two* video game at Brookhaven National Laboratory in Upton, New York. Two people played the electronic tennis game with separate controllers that connected to an analog computer. Using an oscilloscope with an electron beam sweeping across its screen, *Tennis for Two* was the first to entirely show a game's visuals on a screen. Higinbotham was a nuclear physicist who had worked on the Manhattan Project. He never applied for a patent on this first video game.

Voting Machine

The first voting machine was a lever-type device known as the Myers Automatic Booth invented by American Jacob H. Myers and put into use on April 12, 1892, at Lockport, New York, in a local election. Inside a curtained privacy booth, the voter pulled down selected levers to indicate his candidate choices. When the voter finished voting, he opened the privacy curtain with a handle. That caused the voted levers to automatically return to their original horizontal position. Interlocks in the machine prevented the voter from voting for more choices than was permitted.

Vulcanized Rubber

In 1839, Charles Goodyear of New York, New York, discovered the first vulcanized rubber. Goodyear had carelessly dropped some rubber mixed with sulfur on a hot stove, where it charred like leather. He discovered that if he removed the sulfur from rubber and then heated the rubber, the rubber would retain its elasticity. This process, called vulcanization, made rubber water- and winter-proof and, thus, a very marketable product. Goodyear did not patent his invention until June 15, 1844.

War Correspondent

From 1846 to 1850, American George Wilkins Kendall wrote daily stories of his experiences as a volunteer during the Mexican War. He sent his firsthand accounts back by private courier to the *Picayune*, a newspaper in New Orleans, Louisiana, he had cofounded. Kendall had volunteered to be in a Texas Ranger company that was attached to General Zachary Taylor's army on the Rio Grande. The Rangers ran long and dangerous reconnaissance missions, and as a participant, Kendall's in-the-field reporting and firsthand accounts of the war brought himself and his paper immediate fame.

Washing Machine

The first clothes-washing machine was invented in 1677 by Sir John Hoskins of England, a philosopher and lawyer who devoted the latter part of his life to experiments and tinkering. His washing machine used a wheel and cylinder to squeeze water through a coarse-weaved bag of soapy linens. It wrung out the dirty water, cleaning the clothes. The clothes were then removed from the bag and hung to dry.

Water Mill

According to a poem by early Greek writer Antipater, the first water mill dates to about 4000 B.C.E. The poem tells of the water mill providing freedom from the toil of young women who operated small hand mills to grind corn. The first waterwheels, the energy-generating point of water mills, were grindstones mounted atop vertical shafts. The horizontal wheel contained paddled slats that dipped into a swift stream and made the wheel turn. In the first century, the horizontal waterwheels were replaced by vertical ones, which greatly improved the transfer of the water current's power to the milling mechanism. The water mills were used for crop irrigation, to grind grains, and to supply drinking water to villages.

Water Supply System

The Assyrians were the first to use aqueducts, but the ancient Romans were the first to consider the sanitation of their water supply as early as 100 C.E. The notable water commissioner of the era was Sextus Julius Frontinus, who left a detailed account of the water system of Rome. His *De aquae ductu Urbis Romae* (*The Aqueducts of Rome*) talks about the aqueducts bringing in the clean waters of the Apennine Mountains. Settling basins and filters along the main routes helped ensure the clarity of the water.

Wax Museum

The world's first wax museum, Madame Tussauds, was founded in 1835 at the Baker Street Bazaar in London, England, by French-born Marie Grosholtz and her sons. For the preceding 33 years, Grosholtz had been taking her wax exhibitions on tour in the British Isles. She created her first wax figure of Voltaire in 1777, and in 1795, she married Francois Tussaud, which lent a new name to the traveling show. Madame Tussauds, which is still in existence and now boasts numerous other locations, has grown to be the world's largest wax museum, with nearly 400 figures on display at the London museum.

Weather Balloon

On November 21, 1783, the first observation or weather balloon was launched, immediately before the first manned balloon flight, by Frenchmen Jean-François de Rozier and the Marquis d'Aalandes. Measuring about 6 to 8 feet across and filled with hot air, this first weather balloon was used to gauge wind gusts and directions before the manned balloon took flight a little later. More than 100 years later, in 1896, French meteorologist Leon Teisserenc de Bort conducted experiments with high-flying instrumented hydrogen-filled balloons. In 1902, after making 236 flights, most at night, he announced that the atmosphere comprises two layers—the troposphere and stratosphere.

Weather Forecast

Around 650 B.C.E., the Babylonians attempted to predict the weather using both cloud patterns and astrology. The ancients usually relied on observing reoccurring events such as lunar eclipses to make their forecasts. Or if the sunset was particularly red, they observed, the next day often brought fair weather. They also thought that if it were unseasonably warm and sunny in times of winter, snowfall would soon follow in the days ahead. These first weather forecasts were not extremely accurate.

Weather Vane

The first known weather vane dates to the first century B.C.E. Bronze and in the shape of the Greek sea god Triton, complete with the tail of a fish and the upper body of a man, the vane was affixed to the top of the Tower of the Winds, a marble octagon 42 feet high located in Athens, Greece. Astronomer Andronicus of Cyrrhus had built the tower, also called the Horologium, and equipped it with the rotating vane on top to show the direction of the wind. The Horologium was also used to keep time using a sundial on the exterior and a water clock within.

Website

On August 6, 1991, the first website, nxoc01.cern.ch, was launched. It was built at CERN (European Organization for Nuclear Research), initiated by Tim Berners-Lee and Robert Cailliau, developers of the World Wide Web. This first website provided an explanation of what exactly the World Wide Web was and provided instructions on how you could own a browser and set up a web server. This first website also became the world's first web directory, where Berners-Lee maintained a list of other websites in addition to his own.

Wheelbarrow

The wheelbarrow was invented around 400 B.C.E., probably in ancient Greece. Although not called a wheelbarrow, it was described as such an implement among the building material inventories for the temple of Eleusis. The inventories showed "1 body for a one-wheeler (hyperteria monokyklou)." Historians assume it was a singular wooden-wheeled device with a makeshift platform and handles, developed as an innovative technological device by the ancient Greeks. The Romans and the Chinese adopted the wheelbarrow later, making improvements for use in farming, in mining, and as a construction-carrying helper for light loads.

Wimbledon Championship

In July 1877, the first Wimbledon tennis championship was held at the All England Club outside London. The only event was the Gentleman's Singles, which was won by Britain's Spencer Gore. He won the title from a field of 22 contestants by defeating William Marshal 6–1, 6–2, 6–4 in the finals. The gentlemen played on the main grass or Centre Court that was situated in the middle of the grounds. They wore all white and long pants. About 200 spectators paid 1 shilling each to watch. The Wimbledon Championships have been an ongoing annual event ever since.

Women's Golf Tournament

In January 1811, the first women's golf tournament was held at the Royal Musselburgh Golf Club in Musselburgh, Scotland. It was played on the club's putting course and was among the town's fishwives, who because they did the work of men were allowed to play golf. The club arranged to present a special honor award of a new Creel and Skull (fishing basket) to the best female golfer. Other prizes included two of the best Barcelona silk handkerchiefs. The first winner is not known nor is the number of participants. Although the club's intention was to conduct it as an annual event, the tournament did not ultimately catch on.

Women's Professional Sports Team

In 1867, the Dolly Vardens from Philadelphia, Pennsylvania, became the first women's professional sports team. (A dolly varden was a fancy dress named for a character in Charles Dickens's historical novel *Barnaby Rudge: A Tale of the Riots of 'Eighty*.) The Dolly Vardens, an all–African American professional baseball team, were the first paid baseball team on any level, men or women. They played 2 years before the first men's professional club, the Cincinnati Red Stockings. The Dolly Vardens folded after a short time due to lack of support, only to be revived in the late 1880s wearing red calico attire.

Word Processor

Word processing, as it's known today, was first brought about in 1964 with IBM's MT/ST (Magnetic Tape/Selectric Typewriter). With this typewriter, IBM's strategy was first to market the phrase *word processing machine*. The MT/ST used magnetic tape, the first reusable storage medium for typed information. Thanks to the tape, typed data could be edited without having to retype the whole text. Info could be stored on the tape, corrected as needed, and reprinted as many times as desired.

The tape could also be erased and reused for other word processing. Although the first word processor was mainly a business application, average consumers could get one, too.

World Map

Around 540 B.C.E., Anaximander, a philosopher from Miletus, now in Turkey, created the first map of the known world. His innovation represented the entire inhabited land known to the ancient Greeks. The map was circular and showed three continents—Europe, Asia, and Libya (the part of the then-known African continent)—with oceans surrounding the circular map's boundary. Three spokes of water—the Nile River, the Phasis River (now called the Rioni), and the Mediterranean Sea—all emptied into the oceans surrounding the map's perimeter. This first world map was probably engraved on a clay tablet.

World Population Exceeding 1 Billion

The first time the world's population exceeded 1 billion was in 1804, according to reports later compiled using fertility and mortality rates. By 1927, it exceeded 2 billion. The 3 billion milestone was reached in 1960. In 1974, it hit 4 billion. By 1987, the earth held 5 billion people. Twelve years later, in 1999, the population topped 6 billion. It's expected to surpass the 7 billion mark in 2013 and 8 billion in 2028.

World's Fair

In 1851, the Great Exhibition of the Works of Industry of all Nations was housed in the Crystal Palace and other facilities in Hyde Park, London, England. Called the World's Fair by English poet and novelist William Makepeace Thackeray, the event, which ran from May 1 to

October 15, attracted more than 6 million visitors and featured 14,000 exhibitors. The culture and industry gala had the backing of Prince Albert, the husband of Queen Victoria. This first World's Fair made a surplus of money that was used to found three museums plus future educational trusts to provide grants and scholarships for research.

X-Ray

Over the weekend of November 8, 1895, Wilhelm Roentgen of
Wurzburg, Germany, made the first refined discovery of x-radiation.
During an experiment, Roentgen, the first to systematically study
and achieve results from the works of others in the field, covered an
electrified cathode ray tube with a lightproof cardboard black jacket.

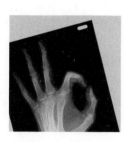

Meanwhile, a screen of fluorescent material lay
on a table a few feet away. While passing an
electrical discharge through the tube, Roentgen
suddenly noticed a shimmering light on the
tabletop. He correctly deducted that the glow
was caused by an unknown high-energy radiation
emitted from the tube.

On December 28, 1895, he published his report, "On a New Kind of
Rays," in the Proceedings of the Physical Medical Society of Wurzburg.
That announcement was illustrated with the first x-ray photograph,
which was of his wife's left hand. The bones could be identified within,
as could the two rings on one of her fingers.

Xylophone

The first xylophone-like percussion instrument existed in the Hindu
regions of southeast Asia around 2000 B.C.E. It originated from *grap*,
wooden keys or slats used to keep rhythm. These keys, made in different

sizes of hardwood or bamboo, were laid on two tracks with a support holding them in such a way to allow tones to flow freely. A heavy string was threaded through holes in the ends of the keys, and the entire keyboard was hung on a stand. A mixture of lead shavings and beeswax in varying thicknesses on the bottom of the keys yielded different tones as the keys were struck. Long, slender beaters with knobs on each end, one for each hand of which melodies could be created, were used to strike the keys and produce the sound.

Yacht

The first yachts are credited to the ancient Egyptians as early as 3000 B.C.E. Those early vessels were made of wood and constructed for the pharaohs to use to sail the Nile River in the afterlife. The yachts, which measured from as short as 8 feet to as long as elegant slender-oared barges 130 feet long, were specially built in the same regal style as the vessels a pharaoh used to cruise the Nile while he was alive. They were carefully fitted together without the use of nails, and because wood was scarce, such vessels were most certainly a royal prerogative. The stocked luxury yachts were buried alongside their pharaohs to provide passage throughout the heavens.

Yo-Yo

Around 500 B.C.E. in ancient Greece, the first yo-yo was made of wood, metal, and terra cotta (clay). The Greeks decorated the two halves, especially the terra cotta ones, with picture-paintings of their gods. The

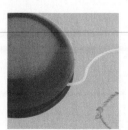

Greeks called them play discs, and they operated pretty much the same as the yo-yos of today, complete with twine. It was customary that when a child turned a certain age, the toys of their youth were offered to certain gods. That meant as a right of passage into adulthood, the Greek children placed their yo-yos on the family altar to pay homage.

included chained-up lions, tigers, bears, wolves, and elephants. Birds were also caged. Shulgi fathered more than 50 children, and it was noted that several of them loved the zoo.

Zipper

In 1851, Elias Howe of Spencer, Massachusetts (and of sewing-machine-inventor fame), was granted a patent for his version of the zipper. Although Howe decided not to commercialize his "automatic, continuous clothing closure," as he called it, his device was the predecessor of later and improved zippers. Howe's zipper was a crude device that had no slider. Instead, it used a series of clasps that slid freely along both edges and joined by a string. By pulling the string taut, the clasps became evenly spaced along the closure, holding the edges together. To open it, one would pull the string in the other direction, which allowed the clasps to become bunched up at one end to be undone. The term *zipper* did not come about until 1925 or 1926 with later, improved versions.

Zoo

Around 2100 B.C.E., King Shulgi of the third dynasty of Ur, or what is now southeast Iraq, established the earliest known zoo. His collections of exotic animals became prized trophies of war gathered for him by his

conquering armies, and he also sent out expeditions to seek new additions. Although this earliest zoo was not open to the public, it was something for Shulgi to boast and brag about to neighboring kingdoms. A zoo was a measure of power, prestige, and wealth. His zoo was a makeshift collection of caves, pens, and roped-off areas and

Index of Topics

Gender and Ethnicity

Government

Health and Beauty

History

Technology

Television

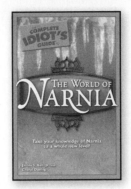

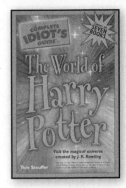

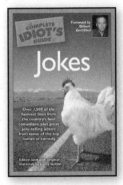